150 best
tagine
recipes

150 best tagine recipes

Including tantalizing recipes for spice blends and accompaniments

Pat Crocker

Robert
ROSE

For complete cataloguing information, see page 224.

Disclaimer

The recipes in this book have been carefully tested by our kitchen and our tasters. To the best of our knowledge, they are safe and nutritious for ordinary use and users. For those people with food or other allergies, or who have special food requirements or health issues, please read the suggested contents of each recipe carefully and determine whether or not they may create a problem for you. All recipes are used at the risk of the consumer.

We cannot be responsible for any hazards, loss or damage that may occur as a result of any recipe use.

For those with special dietary needs, allergies, requirements or health problems, in the event of any doubt, please contact your medical adviser prior to the use of any recipe.

Design and Production: Daniella Zanchetta/PageWave Graphics Inc.
Editor: Carol Sherman
Copy Editor: Karen Campbell-Sheviak
Photographer (food): Colin Erricson
Associate Photographer (food): Matt Johannsson
Food Stylist: Kathryn Robertson
Prop Stylist: Charlene Erricson
Illustrations: Kveta/Three in a Box

Cover image: Chicken with Dried Fruit and Peppers (page 61)

We acknowledge the financial support of the Government of Canada through the Book Publishing Industry Development Program (BPIDP) for our publishing activities.

Published by Robert Rose Inc.
120 Eglinton Avenue East, Suite 800, Toronto, Ontario, Canada M4P 1E2
Tel: (416) 322-6552 Fax: (416) 322-6936
www.robertrose.ca

Printed and bound in Canada

1 2 3 4 5 6 7 8 9 TCP 19 18 17 16 15 14 13 12 11

To the indigenous Berbers and to Arabs, Persians and Andalusians, who influenced the cuisine of Morocco.

"La cuisine, c'est l'ame parfumée de notre culture."
[Cuisine is the perfumed soul of our culture.]

– Edmond Amran el Maleh, (1917)
preeminent Moroccan thinker, writer, teacher of philosophy

Contents

Acknowledgments

L IKE THE MANY cultures of the Maghreb, this book is a melting pot of talents from several professionals. To the account team at Robert Rose and the talented designers at PageWave Graphics, including Daniella Zanchetta, thank you for the deftness with which you plan and execute my books.

Carol Sherman is a perfectionist and the perfect editor. Jensena Campbell, Dawn Tyson, David Hale and Raffi Kouyoumdjian paved the way for testing every tagine recipe in this book, and I am grateful to each of you for supporting this endeavor.

From Olivado Canada, Kim Hannam, I am happily using only avocado oil for high heat cooking. Beretta Organic Farms provides drug-free meats that graze on crops that are not sprayed with chemicals, not genetically modified and are not artificially fertilized. These are the best possible meat products to use in tagine cooking.

I have a network of organic farmers whose produce is used in every recipe, in every book I write, and I would like to thank them for the important work that they do. As always, my beautiful family joins me in judging the dishes and their opinions are woven into every word I write.

Introduction

THE NORTH AFRICAN countries of Algeria, Morocco, Tunisia and Libya are often referred to as the *Maghreb*, or the land where the sun sets. This is because for 7th century Arab conquerors, that part of the Mediterranean lay far to the west of their own Damascus, Baghdad and Cairo.

Many cultures converge in the Maghreb, giving its food the taste of history in every bite. In fact, the cuisines of North Africa may very well be the "melting pot" of the ancient culinary world. The subtle juxtaposition of meat with fruit; the variety and combinations of freshly ground seasonings in a single dish; the delicate sauces and tenderness of tagine dishes — all are a distillation of culinary skills developed over centuries of cooking for kings, armies, nomads and a sophisticated merchant elite.

As part of the Mediterranean basin, North Africa's culinary legacy is one of healthy whole foods — fresh vegetables, legumes, fruit, grains, and olive oils dominate, leaving fish, poultry and dairy products to play secondary, supporting roles. Meat and meat products are consumed the least. Although Muslims avoid wine, moderate consumption of red wine with the main meal of the day is part of the healthy Mediterranean diet.

Mediterranean vegetables, such as eggplant, broad beans, fennel, kohlrabi, lentils and legumes, garlic, red peppers, tomatoes, squash, mushrooms, spinach, vine leaves, garlic and other members of the onion family, are popular. Ground walnuts with chicken; almonds, pine and pistachio nuts in rice dishes; hazelnuts for savory stuffing; and toasted sesame seeds are common in dishes from the region. Nuts are favored in rice as well as in sweetmeats such as halvah and baklava.

The ancient Arabs perfected the distillation process. We still use their word, *al'kahal* (alcohol) for rendering the fragrances of flowers. Rose, orange, and jasmine waters gently infuse rice, sweet pastries, salads, puddings and some vegetable dishes.

Olives and olive oil play a significant role in the kitchen. Traditional North African cooking used *smen*, a strong-tasting, aged butter, or other animal fats although for health reasons, avocado or olive oil is now replacing those staples. Bread or *khobz*, the flatbread of the Moors, is included with almost every meal. Fish is eaten fresh and often in a week, whereas meats such as chicken, lamb or goat may only appear for feasts or special occasions.

In tandem with fresh fruits, vegetables and grains, all of the mysterious spices — those barks, berries, seeds, roots, flowers, translucent resins, bulbs, buds and petals that were transported by the nomadic Berbers — are used with a deftness inherited from generations of use. Indeed, tastes of the Kasbah rely on subtle blends of herbs and spices (up to as many as one hundred in the celebrated Ras el Hanout, page 50) that are still available in much the same form as they were to cooks centuries before the Middle Ages.

> *…candied apple, quince, and plum,*
>   *and gourd;*
> *With jellies smoother than the*
>   *creamy curd;*
> *And lucent syrops, tinct with cinnamon;*
> *Manna and dates… and spiced*
>   *dainties, every one*
> *From silken Samarcand to cedar'd*
>   *Lebanon*
>
> *The Eve of St. Agnes,* **Keats**

Tagine (*tajine* or *tãgin*) Cooking

NORTH AFRICAN CUISINE is more than a combination of the fresh ingredients for which is it known. It is unique because of the equipment and techniques of the Maghreb, foodways that were already in place by the time the Queen of Sheba brought spices to King Solomon. It is steeped in traditions as old as water, and the ancient tools, equipment and techniques transform exotic ingredients into dishes as enduring as the desert's shifting sands. The result is a legion of poetic dishes created for kings, influenced by waves of conquering armies, and passed along throughout history by way of family customs.

In my view, the one important utensil essential to authentic Maghreb dishes is the tagine, a rustic, earthenware, two-piece cooking pot that I like to think may have been handled by Alexander the Great. The word tagine may refer to either the two-part, domed earthenware dish or the slow-cooked stews that result in luscious, complex-flavored, moist and tender combinations of delicately spiced meat and/or vegetables with fruit or nuts or grains. And while tagine "pots" may be used throughout the Maghreb region, they are most often associated with Moroccan cuisine.

When a tagine pot is used for cooking, the resulting dish is rich in concentrated sweet, sour and savory flavors in a velvet-smooth sauce. The upswept shape of the tagine lid allows moisture and steam to circulate up and around the food so it poaches as it cooks and becomes incredibly tender. The closest Western cooking technique to that of the tagine is braising meats and vegetables in liquid.

In Morocco and Algeria, small braziers are banked with charcoal and lit so the heat from the embers cooks the food in the clay tagine slowly and evenly. The long, slow, moist cooking technique is the secret to the deep rich flavors that only tagine pots, with their uniquely shaped lids, can produce.

Tagine Know-How

Traditional Tagine Pots

Traditional Moroccan clay tagines are made today in much the same way as they have been for centuries. Fashioned of terra cotta, which usually boasts a dull red clay finish, some are crude and unadorned; others are glazed and brightly decorated, some with gems and silver, on the outside of the lid. The traditional tagine (or *tāgin* as the Berbers call the pot) is never glazed on the inside of the lid because condensed liquids escape slowly from an unglazed tagine lid, giving the food inside a more concentrated flavor spike. Glazing may be added to the outside of the lid or the inside and/or outside of the bottom section. The delicate clay is susceptible to cracking, chipping and breaking and must be treated gently. It can never be placed on direct heat on top of the stove or subjected to extreme temperature changes. While some cooks claim that they use an authentic clay Berber tagine pot on top of a gas stove but only with a heat diffuser, I recommend that the only safe way to use these pots is in a medium oven (350°F/180°C).

A Word of Caution: Some highly decorated clay tagine pots are made from clay that is toxic or not safe to use with heat. Avoid cooking or serving food in clay pots that are not accompanied with cooking and food use instructions.

Modern Tagines

Western cookware manufacturers are producing modern adaptations of the Berber clay tagine using tempered stoneware, cast-iron and clay materials. These "new" tagines allow for safe stovetop tagine cooking. In fact, modern tagine pots are designed for use primarily on top of a gas or electric element. While they may also be used in the oven, stovetop cooking in a tagine takes less time than cooking the same recipe in the oven. For this reason, most of the recipes in this book take advantage of the shorter, stovetop method.

Today's tagine pots have a wide, shallow base made from cast iron or flameproof stoneware or unique clay that conducts heat slowly and evenly over gas or electric elements, rendering them flexible and convenient for Western cooks. Some are made to be used in the microwave as well as in the oven and on the stovetop and a few are dishwasher safe.

Modern tagines have the same conical shaped lid as the ancient clay pots because they make use of the traditional wide, shallow base and tall lid for their steam and moist heat cooking results. However, each brand has a slightly different height and width to the base and cone and employs different materials. What follows is a review of the top tagine brands, with notes on how to use the recipes in this book with each.

Caution: Check manufacturer's instructions on the care and use of your new tagine pot before using it.

Notes on the Most Popular Tagine Brands

Brand	Emile Henry	Le Creuset
Stovetop?	Yes, safe on all heat sources*; raised feet on bottom; induction disk available for induction stovetop Use only over medium-low to low stovetop heat	Yes, safe on any heat source*; flat base; may scratch glass tops May use high heat, but follow recipe instructions
Microwave?	Yes	No
Oven?	Yes	Yes
Freezer?	Yes, check manufacturer's instructions	Yes, check manufacturer's instructions
Dishwasher?	Yes, presoak burnt-on food residue or use gentle cleaning materials	Yes, but hand wash is recommended; use gentle materials
Materials	**Base:** "Flame"© (heat resistant) ceramic **Lid:** glazed ceramic **Color:** various	**Base:** vitreous matte black enamel-coated cast iron **Lid:** glazed ceramic **Color:** black base; various colors of lids
Size, base	**Large:** 3½ quart (3.5 L); 13.7-inch (35 cm) diameter; 3 inches (7.5 cm) deep **Height, base + lid:** 9 inches (23 cm) **Medium:** 2½ quart (2.5 L); 12.5-inch (32 cm) diameter; 2.3 inches (6 cm) deep **Height, base + lid:** 8.2 inches (21 cm) **Small:** 1½ quart (1.5 L); 10.2-inch (26 cm) diameter; 1.5 inches (4 cm) deep **Height, base + lid:** 6.6 inches (17 cm)	**Medium:** 2 quart (1.9 L); 8.6-inch (22 cm) diameter; 2.3 inches (6 cm) deep **Height, base + lid:** 9 inches (23 cm)
Attributes	Excels at oven-cooking; with use, thin cracks may appear in the glaze, this is not a flaw	Cast iron provides even, slow heat conductivity; the base stays hot at the table for up to 1 hour; base can be used on its own on top or in the oven or under a grill
Cooking with this brand:	Use a slightly lower temperature (base may develop "hot spots," which burn food if too high temperature is used); use less liquid; sauté onions 1 or 2 minutes longer; stir more often than called for in recipes in this book. If you wish to brown meat, use a skillet or sauté pan for this purpose and transfer the meat to the bottom of the tagine and complete the recipe.	Base is deep but still it is a Small to Medium size, so use only recipes that call for a Small tagine or reduce ingredients by about one-quarter when a Medium tagine is called for; use heat and liquid as recommended in the recipes in this book.

Brand	Maxwell & Williams	Staub
Stovetop?	Yes, safe on any heat source*; raised feet on bottom Use only over medium to low stovetop heat	Yes, safe on any heat source*; flat, enamel base May use high heat, but follow recipe instructions
Microwave?	Yes	No
Oven?	Yes	Yes
Freezer?	Yes, check manufacturer's instructions	Yes
Dishwasher?	Yes	Yes, but it is recommended to follow use and care instructions
Materials	**Base:** flameproof stoneware with Microstoven© nonstick finish **Lid:** glazed ceramic **Color:** various	**Base:** enameled black matte over cast iron **Lid:** glazed ceramic **Color:** black base, cream lid
Size, base	**Large:** only available in Australia **Medium:** 1$\frac{1}{4}$ quart (1.25 L) capacity; 9.6 inches (24.5 cm) diameter; 1.9 inches (5 cm) deep **Height, base + lid:** 9.8 inches (25 cm) **Small:** $\frac{1}{2}$ quart (.5 L) capacity; 6-inch (15 cm) diameter; 1.7 inches (4.5 cm) deep **Height, base + lid:** 7.6 inches (19.5 cm) **Mini:** only available in Australia	**Medium:** 2$\frac{3}{4}$ quart (2.75 L); 9.8-inch (25 cm) diameter; 2.3 inches (6 cm) deep **Height, base + lid:** 8.2 inches (21 cm)
Attributes	Even heat distribution; stays hot up to 45 minutes; microwaveable; easy to clean	Even heat distribution prevents burning; browns, braises and reduces liquids well; retains heat for up to 1 hour
Cooking with this brand:	Follow recipes in this book and you should not have to make adjustments	Follow recipes in this book and you should not have to make adjustments

*Heat Sources: gas, electric radiant or electric solid plates; ceramic, halogen, induction stoves

Stovetop Browning

Many recipes for North American stew or ragoût require initial browning of the meat for long, slow, moist heat cooking or braising. While high-heat searing or browning does not seal in the juice, it does add to the rich, caramelized taste of the meats and gives them an attractive browned finish.

If you wish to brown beef, poultry and lamb before combining it with the other ingredients for cooking it in a tagine, you may do this as a preliminary step. Only those tagines with a cast-iron or special flameproof stoneware base will brown meat satisfactorily. This is because despite the flameproof capability of some tagine bottoms, ceramic pots simply do not brown food well. If you want to brown meat and own a flameproof ceramic tagine, use a skillet or sauté pan for this purpose and transfer the meat to the bottom of the tagine and complete the recipe.

Can I use my tagine on top of the stove?

Yes, but only if it is labeled as being "flameproof." Most modern ceramic, stoneware and all stainless-steel and cast-iron tagine bottoms may be used directly on electric or gas elements. Some specially marked ceramic or stoneware tagines (such as the Emile Henry and Maxwell Williams tagines) may be placed over direct heat but most others must be used in tandem with a heat diffuser. Check the manufacturer's instructions before using your tagine on top of the stove.

Stovetop vs. Oven Cooking

Because all modern flameproof tagines are meant for use on top of the stove, most of the recipes in this book use a stovetop method, but you will find a few recipes that require the dish to bake in the oven. Of course, all of the recipes in this book may be easily converted to the oven cooking method. To do this, simply use a skillet to sauté or brown vegetables or meat and transfer those ingredients to the tagine bottom. Add remaining ingredients, cover and bake in a 350°F (180°C) oven for about twice as long as the stovetop method suggests, or until the degree of tenderness described in the recipe is reached.

Which is better: stovetop or oven for cooking tagines?

Stovetop cooking in a tagine is generally faster than using an oven and the stovetop method is best for the tender cuts of meat. Fish, seafood, vegetables, tender beef and lamb and poultry are ideal for stovetop tagine cooking. To brown meat and sauté vegetables, medium heat is recommended. Once the vegetables and other ingredients are added to the base of the tagine, the lid is secured and the heat is reduced to low. Usually less liquid is used for the stovetop methods and no extra liquid is required, even after longer cooking. Sometimes water will appear on the bottom rim. This is condensed steam and to release it, simply remove the lid for a few seconds, replace and continue cooking.

Cooking with a tagine in the oven takes a minimum of 1 hour and up to 3 hours to cook some of the tougher cuts of meat such as shoulder and shank lamb and beef. The moist, slow cooking technique is an ideal way to ensure that the tougher cuts of meat are tender and richly sauced. Slightly more broth or water is added when cooking with a tagine in the oven, and sometimes more liquid may be needed during the cooking from time to time, so it is advised to occasionally check on liquid levels in tagines when using the oven.

Glazing

As mentioned previously, traditional earthenware tagine lids are not glazed on the inside so that as the steam escapes, the remaining sauce and food becomes intensely flavored, tender and melded in taste and texture. Tagines with glazed lids allow steam to collect on the lid, condense back into liquid and drip into the cooking sauce. This has the advantage of providing a moist heat that poaches the meat. If your tagine lid is glazed on the inside — it will be smooth to the touch and shiny — you may notice a build-up of water on the lip of the tagine bottom as food simmers on low. To dissipate the condensed water, lift the lid and it will disappear. Since most of the modern tagines available in North America have glazed lids, the recipes in this book use slightly less liquid than recipes intended for tagines with unglazed lids.

What to do if there is too much liquid after cooking?

The first time you use your tagine will be a test for its slow-cooking characteristics. See individual brand characteristics (pages 12 and 13) to determine if recipes in this book need to be slightly adjusted for your tagine.

If the amount of sauce or liquid in the bottom of the tagine is thin, bland tasting or too abundant, if tagine base is cast iron or special stoneware, remove meat and bring liquids to a boil over high heat, reduce heat to medium and lightly boil until the sauce is slightly thickened and reduced to the desired consistency. If using a flameproof ceramic tagine, transfer the liquid to a heavy-bottomed saucepan, bring to a boil over high heat, reduce heat to medium-high and lightly boil until the sauce is slightly thickened and reduced to the desired consistency. Now you have an idea of how much liquid your tagine requires and can adjust the recipes in this book accordingly so that this step is not required.

Hole in the Lid

A few manufacturers incorporate a hole in the lid of their tagines in order to allow for escaping steam that builds up during cooking. Traditional tagines do not have a hole in the lid because the unglazed clay allows steam to pass through without building up inside the pot. Only those tagine pots that are constructed of non-porous materials may require a hole in the lid. If you are using a tagine with a hole in the lid, check the liquid at least once during cooking to be sure that it is not too dry.

My tagine does not have a hole in the lid. Do I need to lift the lid occasionally during cooking?

No. Manufacturers who design and fabricate modern tagines have tested their product and know that the materials are heat safe. If your tagine does not have a hole in the lid, you can be assured that there will be no dangerous build-up of steam while the food inside simmers. If your tagine lid is glazed on the inside — it will be smooth to the touch and shiny — you may notice a build-up of water on the lip of the tagine bottom as food simmers on low. To dissipate the condensed water lift the lid and it will disappear.

Tagines as Serving Utensils

Moroccans often cook couscous separately and serve tagine-cooked food with it. The main course foods are brought to the table on a platter or in a separate or serving tagine bottom. There is a wide variety of clay tagines that are not heatproof that are used only for table presentation. That is, cooked food is transferred to the tagine before serving. Before using a clay tagine for serving food, check to be sure that it is food safe.

Most modern tagines are designed as oven-to-tableware and complement Western décor and table settings. As with all ceramic oven dishes, earthenware, clay or ceramic tagines removed from the oven should not be set directly on countertops or other cool surfaces. The sudden contact with a cold surface may cause cracks or, worse, breakage.

Modern Features

While traditional earthenware tagine pots may not have changed in centuries of use by North African cooks, modern tagines are constantly being improved by North American manufacturers. Some have a nonstick finish on the interior of the base unit, while others are being offered in a variety of colors and sizes, including mini or individual-serving sizes.

How can I use small or mini-size tagines?

These beautiful, petite tagines are perfect for cooking warm dips and individual, appetizer-size savory dishes for the start of a meal. I have developed some dessert, dip and starter tagine recipes that may be cooked and served in individual-serving size tagines.

Where can I buy a tagine?

Most specialty food stores and department stores with a kitchen equipment section sell food-grade tagines. If you purchase a pottery tagine from a home decorating store, unless it comes with cooking instructions, it was not meant as a cooking vessel. You must also be sure to determine if it is food safe before serving food in it.

North African Flavor Footprint

Herbs & Spices

Caraway *Carum carvi*

Arguably one of the world's oldest culinary spices, with evidence of seeds found in the remains of food from the Mesolithic age about 5,000 years ago. The Ancient Egyptians always placed a container of caraway in tombs to ward off evil spirits. Caraway seeds are mericarps that split into two crescent-shaped brown seeds with five tan-colored ridges.

caraway

How to describe the tastes of North Africa? In this book, I will begin with magical spice route ingredients, whose properties are the stuff of myths and legends: cinnamon, pepper, lemons, saffron, sesame, ruby-seeded pomegranates, figs, turmeric, dates, olives and more.

The tastes of North Africa rely on a subtle play of spicy balanced with sour, fruity and sweet ingredients. The Persian influence is found in the sour tastes (from tamarind, capers, sumac, lemons and vinegar) that are subtly combined with fresh or preserved fruit and the sweetness of honey, dates and figs. Present day recipes with piquant sumac, dried limes, preserved lemons, pickled capers or pomegranate are surely a throwback to 500 BC when the Persian Empire enveloped the whole region.

Culinary: Used in soups, vegetable dishes, spice blends and in teas. It aids digestion and is often served at the end of the meal along with anise seeds.

Medicinal: Caraway has long been used to comfort babies with gas because it aids digestion.

Taste: A taste of anise with a hint of eucalyptus and a warm, sweet and slightly peppery aroma.

Cardamom *Elettaria cardamomum*

Thought to have grown in the gardens of Babylon, cardamom comes from the Greek word, *kardamomum*, meaning very spicy. A rhizomatous perennial with large lanceolate leaves and striking white flowers with dark pink stripes, it is similar in appearance to ginger or lily plants.

Originally from Indian rainforests, cardamom grows wild in southern India, Sri Lanka, Thailand, Tanzania and Central America.

cardamom

Taste: Pungent with overtones of camphor and eucalyptus, with lime or astringent qualities; overall, warm and refreshing.

Culinary: The black, brown, or green seeds inside the pods are used in many spice blends and as a flavoring for the rich dark espresso-like coffee of the region. Sometimes the whole pod is used in a blend that is crushed to a powder.

Medicinal: Tonic; antispasmodic and carminative; cardamom relaxes spasms, stimulates appetite and relieves flatulence.

Chile Peppers *Capsicum annuum* or *C. frutescens*

Many dishes of the Maghreb make extensive use of this fiery herb. Peppers are not native to Europe but were brought to the region from their native South and Central Americas by Spain's conquistadores. There are more than 150 different species of capsicum, with extreme variations in heat from mild to very hot. One of the most common chile peppers in the Maghreb is the slim, red, hot cayenne, although other dried hot chile peppers are often used in Harissa (page 45).

chile peppers

Taste: The characteristic pungency of chiles is caused by the presence of *capsaicin*. Research has shown that the components of *capsaicin* (capsaicinoids) promote different taste sensations when eaten, giving either a short fiery flavor or lingering hot taste.

Culinary: Used fresh or dried, green or red, whole or chopped in sauces and spice blends.

Medicinal: Chiles are rich in vitamin C; stimulate blood circulation; purify the blood; promote fluid elimination and sweating. Cayenne is most often used as a stimulating nerve tonic.

Cinnamon *Cinnamomum zeylanicum* and *C. cassia*

Cinnamon has long been associated with ancient rituals of sacrifice or pleasure. The Egyptians used cinnamon in embalming. Hieroglyphics on a temple from around 1489 BC by the Pharaoh queen, Hatshepsut, reveal that she dispatched ships to Punt (now Somalia) for several spices including cinnamon, frankincense and myrrh trees. *Kayu manis* is Malay for "sweet" and is thought to be the origin of the word cinnamon.

The spice we call cinnamon is the bark from tropical evergreen trees related to the bay laurel, avocado and sassafras.

cinnamon

Taste: Sweet, fragrant, warm and aromatic, similar to dry sandalwood.

Culinary: True cinnamon is the lighter, sweeter tasting *C. zeylanicum*, which is soft and lightly perfumed with no trace of bitterness or pungency. *C. cassia* is more commonly sold as powdered cinnamon. It is harder, darker and stronger tasting than *C. zeylanicum*.

Medicinal: A stimulant, astringent and carminative; used to treat nausea, vomiting, diarrhea and stomach upsets. Recent studies indicate that cinnamon helps the body use insulin more efficiently. Oil from the leaves is used as a substitute for clove oil, and oil from the bark is used in the manufacture of perfume.

Cloves *Syzygium aromaticum*

Cloves are the unopened flower buds of a tall, fragrant, evergreen tree that was native and exclusive to the Moluccas (Spice Islands) until early in the 1700s. It is thought that cloves were part of the spices introduced to North African cuisine by Portuguese or Spanish spice traders.

Taste: Slightly astringent; sweetly pungent and lightly fruity but assertive and warm with notes of pepper and camphor.

Culinary: Ground cloves are used in both savory and sweet dishes of North Africa.

Medicinal: Used to treat asthma, bronchitis, nausea, vomiting, flatulence, diarrhea and hypothermia. The *eugenol* in clove oil is a key ingredient in some dentistry products, mouthwash, toothpaste and some soap.

cloves

Coriander *Coriandrum sativum*

Coriander seeds have been found in the tombs of the Pharaohs. The Roman legions carried coriander as they progressed through Europe, using it to flavor their bread. The word comes from the Greek word *koris*, for bed bug, because of the similarity between the smell of the fresh green cilantro leaves and the offending bug.

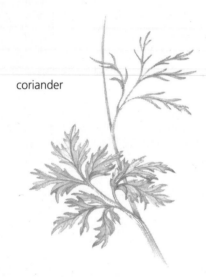

coriander

Taste: The dried seeds have a pleasing, mild, sweet, slightly orange taste. Fresh green leaves are pungent and strongly flavored. Many people cannot use fresh cilantro because of its strong aroma and taste, which to them is soap-like and inedible.

Culinary: Coriander seeds are frequently combined with cumin seeds, the two spices being toasted together before being ground. Whole coriander is used in tagine dishes and pickles.

Medicinal: Coriander seed oil has antibacterial properties and is included in treatments for colic, neuralgia and rheumatism.

Cumin *Cuminum cyminum*

A native of a specific location in the Nile Valley of Egypt, whole or ground cumin seed is one of the most commonly used spices in North African cuisine. Now cultivated in Morocco, Iran, Turkey, India, China and the Americas, there is evidence that it was used in Egyptian and Minoan medicines from 5,000 years ago. It is mentioned in the Bible and has been a symbol of greed and meanness, or a sign of loyalty.

The plant is a small, herbaceous umbellifer that bears boat-shaped seeds with nine ridges, similar to caraway, but smaller and lighter, with a brown-yellow color.

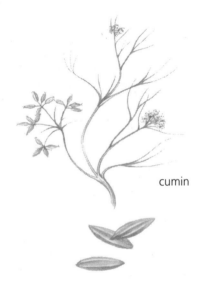

cumin

Taste: Taste is sharp and pungent with a hint of caraway; strong, spicy-sweet aroma. Toasting before grinding brings out a rich, nutty flavor, making the spice less harsh. Less common black Iranian cumin seeds are slightly sweeter and more delicate in flavor.

Culinary: Ground cumin is widely used in Moroccan spice blends and lamb tagines and to flavor some cheeses.

Medicinal: Used in tisanes and aperitifs as an appetite stimulant; widely used as a carminative to ease stomach disorders; and to increase milk in breastfeeding. Cumin oil is used in perfumes.

Fennel *Foeniculum vulgare*

An herb used from antiquity, fennel was believed to have the power to make people young, strong and healthy. A tall, leggy aromatic perennial of the parsley family, fennel is native to Southern Europe and the Mediterranean, where it grows particularly well near the sea. The gray-green, oval seeds with five ridges are harvested when the fruit of the plant matures.

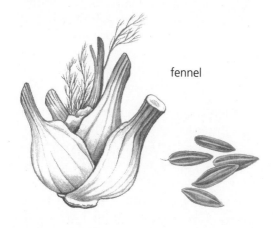

fennel

Taste: Warm, sweet, mildly anise flavor.

Culinary: Crushed seeds are used in savory and sweet baked goods, meats, fish and some vegetable dishes. For a pleasing hint of anise, chop fresh fennel bulb and add 1 cup (250 mL) to any of the tagine recipes in this book.

Medicinal: Used to treat earache, toothache, asthma and rheumatism. Fennel oil is used in cough medicine, licorice sweets, perfumes and soaps.

Fenugreek *Trigonella foenum-graecum*

A small erect and slender annual fodder plant that is similar in appearance to clover. Leaves are light green with three small, oblong leaflets. The plant produces pods that hold between 10 and 20 triangular, light yellow seeds.

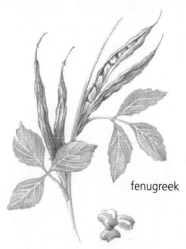

fenugreek

Taste: Most commonly associated with the curry taste; the seeds have a tangy, faint celery flavor, like burnt sugar when toasted; highly aromatic, smelling of curry.

Culinary: The fresh or dried leaves are used when available, but it is the dried seeds that are most commonly used in Middle Eastern cooking. Fenugreek is a key ingredient in curry powder, lending the curry aroma most associated with that blend of spices. The seeds are difficult to grind and may be sprouted and used in salads and breads or soaked overnight to produce a bitter tasting, thick, jellylike substance for drinks, sauces and preserves.

Medicinal: Rich in protein, minerals (including iron) and vitamins, fenugreek seeds are important ingredients in vegetable and tagine dishes because they add nutrients to the diet. Seeds are used to stimulate the metabolism; help control blood-sugar levels in diabetes; assist with stomach and digestive disorders, and lower blood pressure.

Because it protects intestinal surfaces, fenugreek is used in bronchitis, diverticular disease, ulcerative colitis, Crohn's disease and peptic ulcers.

Ginger *Zingiber officinale*

Ginger is a tropical plant with lance-shaped leaves and yellow flowers that produces an edible, fleshy rhizome. The name is believed to come from the Sanskrit *singabera*, meaning "shaped like a horn," evolving to the Greek *zingiberi* and subsequently the Latin *zingiber*. Traded by Arabs, Romans, Portuguese and eventually Spaniards, by the 14th century, ginger became the most common spice after pepper. An essential spice in North African cooking, ginger is, according to the Koran, included on the menu in Paradise.

ginger

Taste: Sharp, citrus flavor that is hot and biting.

Culinary: The essential oil is used in commercial flavorings. Fresh gingerroot is sliced, minced, grated, chopped, crushed or juiced and added to a wide variety of recipes. Dried whole root may be added to pickled vegetables or cooked with tagines and later removed. Ground dried ginger is widely used for baked products, savory recipes and other dishes. Pickled gingerroot is often served with sushi and may be used for a tart flavor in savory dishes. Preserved or stem ginger is boiled in syrup and used in sweet dishes; candied ginger is preserved in a heavy, strong syrup and used with cakes and other baked dishes; and crystallized ginger is cooked in syrup, then dried and rolled in sugar.

Medicinal: Ginger is most effective as an antinausea medication. It stimulates blood flow to the digestive system and increases nutrient absorption. It increases the action of the gallbladder while protecting the liver against toxins and preventing the formation of ulcers.

Mastic *Pistacia lentiscus*

Mastic is a resin from small evergreen trees or bushes growing on the Greek island of Chios. When stems of the trees are punctured, sticky, translucent oval tears of resin appear. The lumps are collected and pulverized in an electric mill or combined with sugar and pounded in a mortar and pestle. Mastic is often confused with gum arabic (a completely different product).

mastic

Nutmeg *Myristica fragrans*

The nutmeg tree is a large evergreen native to the Banda Islands in the Moluccas. It grows to about 60 feet (18 m) and produces fruit only after 15 to 20 years and then produces fruit for 30 to 40 years, often bearing 1,500 to 2,000 fruits per annum. The apricot-like fruit splits when ripe to reveal brilliant red arils encasing the brown nut. The red arils, called mace, turn to an orange color as they dry. The mace is removed from the nut and dried. The nut is also dried until the kernel inside rattles, and is removed by tapping the end of the nutmeg shell.

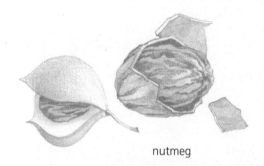

nutmeg

Taste: Light, bitter pine flavor.

Culinary: Mastic is used as a flavoring for Turkish ice cream, milk desserts and in Egypt, with other herbs in chicken broth. A small pinch of ground mastic will be enough to flavor most dishes.

Medicinal: Used for several thousands of years as a medicine for gastrointestinal ailments, science has confirmed that mastic kills the bacterium that causes most peptic ulcers. A team of Canadian and Moroccan ethnobotanists has studied Berberic medicinal plants for their effectiveness in fighting herpes simplex, polio virus and *Sindbis* viruses. Mastic showed antiviral activity against herpes simplex.

Taste: Aromatic, sweet and warm, with a light clove and wood taste. Mace and nutmeg have a similar flavor, with nutmeg being slightly sweeter and richer than mace.

Culinary: Mace is sold as whole blades or as ground spice and is used in savory dishes. Nutmeg may be whole or ground and flavors savory recipes, but is especially complementary to sweet dishes, including puddings, cakes and drinks.

Medicinal: Anti-inflammatory; soothes pain; sedative; nutmeg is astringent, a digestive stimulant and an aphrodisiac. Nutmeg oil is used in perfumes and ointments.

Paprika *Capsicum annuum*

Red bell peppers are ground to a fine powder to produce most of the paprika that is sold in North America. Varying degrees of hot-tasting paprika are made from chile peppers and are available from spice sellers in markets throughout the Middle East. The fruit from the *Capsicum annuum* arrived in Spain after Columbus' voyage in 1492 and it was the Spanish who dried and pounded them for pimentón, or what we know as paprika. While it is the national spice of Hungary, paprika is still grown in Spain and Portugal for export and used all over the Mediterranean and Maghreb regions.

Pepper *Piper nigrum*

The quest for pepper sparked the discovery of the New World and is intertwined (from a Western point of view) with the history of the spice trade itself. Long pepper was described in Sanskrit by the word *pippali*, from which the Greek *peperi*, the Latin *piper* and the English *pepper* are derived.

Peppercorns are the fruit of a perennial tropical vine that grows on taller palm trees. Catkins bear tiny flowers, which produce berries on spikes, generating 50 or more single-seeded fruits that are green (black when dried) or pink in color. Black peppercorns are the most common.

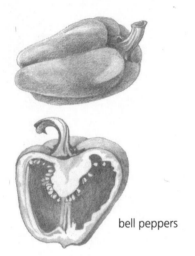

bell peppers

black pepper

Taste: Ranges from smoky-sweet and mild to increasingly hot and pungent.

Culinary: Used as a garnish and in spice blends or alone in savory tagine dishes.

Medicinal: Fresh red peppers are high in vitamin C, however the high temperatures used to dry peppers for paprika destroys the vitamin C but it is still an excellent source of beta-carotene (the precursor to vitamin A), a known antioxidant.

Taste: The pungent taste and biting heat of pepper is determined by its essential oils (found mostly in the hull) and the alkaloid *piperline*, both of which vary by soil and location of where the peppers are grown.

Culinary: Peppercorns are dried and sold whole, cracked, crushed or powdered. They are used in Moroccan spice blends and in savory dishes.

Medicinal: Aids digestion; in a paste with other herbs to treat skin rashes and eczema.

Rose *Rosa species*

Rose imprints on slate deposits in the Florissant Fossil Beds near Cripple Creek, Colorado, have been identified as "wild species" roses and are from 35 to 40 million years old. Wild species roses — the plants from which all modern roses descend — are hardy, with simple single flowers growing on shrubs or climbing cane-like shoots and big hips.

Crusaders, gypsies, artists and artisans spread the reign of the rose from the Middle East, North Africa and Eastern Europe to the Western regions of that continent.

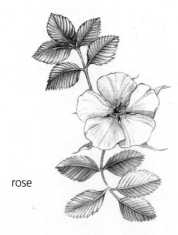

rose

Taste: Aromatic, sweet and intensely fragrant.

Culinary: Rose petals and rose water have played a major role in Arabian food for centuries.

Medicinal: Rose hips are rich in vitamin C (highest in hips from the dog rose) and contain high levels of calcium, phosphorus and iron, making them ideal as winter tonics to help increase the body's resistance to infectious diseases.

Red rose petals from *R. Gallica* are the only recognized petals to be used in medicinal preparations. Rose bark and roots have been used to treat dysentery, diarrhea and worms; a tea of rose petals was once taken as a tonic. Rose water is still used for cosmetics and eye lotions.

Saffron *Crocus sativus*

True saffron comes only from *Crocus sativus*, an autumn flowering, ornamental perennial that grows to about 6 inches (15 cm). In the fall, corms send up solitary flower stalks and then leaves similar to chives, which surround the violet flower. The flower bears six stamen and three styles, each holding a stigma. It is the three bright red stigmas that are hand-plucked and dried.

Saffron's original worth grew out of its color for the Persian carpet industry. Sometime around the Middle Ages, its color and aroma became a status symbol for cloth and culinary dishes. The fact that one flower only produces three stigmas that are hand-harvested makes saffron one of, if not *the* most expensive spice available today.

saffron

Taste: Pungent, bitter, woodsy, flowery.

Culinary: Use 4 to 6 whole filaments per serving as a general rule. To activate and release the aromatic properties of saffron, infuse in warm liquid or gently grind to a powder (it is recommended to always infuse or powder the threads, not to toss directly into a dish as it is cooking).

Medicinal: Ayurvedic medicine uses saffron to treat asthma, coughs, colds and skin diseases. The active ingredient *crocetin* may help reduce cholesterol levels in the blood.

Sesame *Sesamum indicum*

It is not clear whether sesame originated in Africa or India, but in 1500 BC, the Ebers Papyrus lists sesame as *sesemt*. Seeds are sold whole (with hulls); raw (dark); hulled and polished; raw (white); and hulled and roasted (tan).

sesame

Taste: Mild flavor, which develops to a nutty taste when toasted.

Culinary: Plain and toasted sesame oil is used as a cooking medium and as a flavoring for sauces and other dishes; toasted seeds are sprinkled over tagine dishes or pastries as a garnish in Middle Eastern cooking. Seeds are used whole or ground to an oily, beige-colored paste known as tahini, which is used in hummus and other Middle Eastern dips and sauces. The seeds are scattered on bread, sweet and savory crackers, particularly in Greece and Turkey.

Medicinal: High in calcium and a good source of incomplete protein, which combines well with legumes or whole grains. Used in laxatives; as an emollient and in poultices.

Sumac *Rhus coriaria*

Sumac is a 10-foot (3 m) bush with leaves that turn bright red in the fall. The berries are picked before they ripen, dried and crushed to a powder for use on kebabs, fish and in salads. The Romans and Persians used sumac berries as a souring agent, much like we would use lemon juice or vinegar.

sumac

Taste: Astringent, sour fruit flavor with a hint of citrus.

Culinary: Used whole, the berries are cracked and soaked in warm water for 15 to 20 minutes, then squeezed to release their astringent juice, which is added to foods toward the end of the cooking process. Ground sumac is combined with other spices (see Za'atar, page 54), rubbed into meat or fish and the juice is used in sauces, marinades and salad dressings. Widely used in North African and Middle Eastern cuisines.

Medicinal: Often mixed in a drink for upset stomach, and to treat fevers and bowel complaints; said to have diuretic properties.

Turmeric *Curcuma longa*

A robust, fleshy rhizome similar to ginger but slightly thinner and rounder, with a lighter brown skin and brilliant orange-yellow flesh, turmeric is a tall-growing plant with long, flat, bright green leaves growing up from the base.

The name is thought to originate from the Latin, *terra merita* meaning "merit of the earth." Turmeric may have originated in Iran, but India is now the world's largest exporting country (China, Indonesia, Taiwan, Sri Lanka, West Indies, Australia and Peru are also producers).

Tamarind *Tamarindus indica*

The Tamarind is a tall evergreen tree bearing pods with large, hard, shiny beans surrounded by a sour pulp. Arabs call it *thamar-i-hindi*, fruit of India.

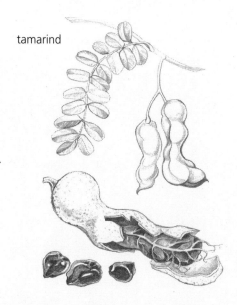

tamarind

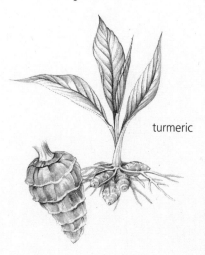

turmeric

Taste: Sour, slightly sweet and fruity.

Culinary: When used with sugar, it imparts a sweet-and-sour flavor to foods. Flavors dipping sauces, pickles, and a key ingredient in Worcestershire sauce. Drinks are made from tamarind syrup.

Tamarind is sold in Indian and Middle Eastern food stores in two forms: semi-dried, a sticky mass of broken pods with fibers and beans; or as a moist vacuum-packed fibrous pulp.

Medicinal: Said to be cooling and cleansing, especially for the liver.

Taste: Earthy, sharp, bitter-spice with citrus notes.

Culinary: Use fresh or ground turmeric as a substitute for saffron; it is featured in curries, Moroccan tagines, with chicken, seafood, lentils and vegetables, in pickles, sauces and rice dishes.

Medicinal: Antioxidant, -inflammatory, -bacterial, -fungal, -microbial and -viral; lowers blood cholesterol; reduces post-exercise pain; heals wounds; protects liver cells. Used to treat rheumatoid arthritis, cancer, candida, AIDS, Crohn's disease, eczema, hepatitis, nausea and digestive disturbances, and it appears to inhibit colon and breast cancers.

Mediterranean Ingredients

Artichokes *Cynara scolymus*

Artichokes are the flowers of a thistle plant and as such, have tough outer leaves and hairy, inedible centers, or chokes. Look for bright green-purple artichokes with no signs of browning and tightly closed leaves.

Taste: Fresh artichokes have a delicate, slightly flowery flavor.

Culinary: Trim away the thick stems and tough outer leaves. Simmer in a saucepan half filled with boiling water and 1 tbsp (15 mL) lemon juice for 20 to 35 minutes or until the outer leaves pull away easily. Cut in half and remove the hairy, inedible center. Canned artichoke hearts are usually marinated and are more flavorful than fresh. Add canned, drained artichoke hearts to cooked tagines at the last minute.

Medicinal: Antioxidant, anticancer, heart protective.

Bulgur

Bulgur is a cracked wheat product that is made by steaming or parboiling, drying and crushing wheat berries. This process makes the hard wheat berries easier and faster to cook. Bulgur is available in fine, medium and coarse grinds. Its flavor is nutty and rich and more distinct than that of couscous. Pure cracked wheat is simply the cracked berries (without the steaming and drying steps), with more of the nutritious bran layers intact. Bulgur and cracked wheat may be used interchangeably in the tagine recipes in this book.

Capers *Capparis spinosa* (wild, spiny variety) or *C. inermis* (cultivated)

Grown extensively throughout the Maghreb and Mediterranean regions, capers are the flower buds of a low-growing bush with round, fairly thick leaves and pink flowers that resemble a simple rose. The short-lived flowers sport long tassels of purple stamens. The flower buds have been used as an ingredient in food since Biblical times.

The small, hard buds are processed by hand — harvested, washed and softened in the sun for a day before being pickled. Capers may be preserved in salt alone or, more commonly, in salted wine vinegar, brine or olive oil.

Taste: Sharp, with a sour bite and salty vinegar flavor.

Culinary: Chopped capers are often used as the sour component in tagine dishes; in sauces such as tartare and rémoulade; in antipasti and salads; as toppings for dishes; and whole as a key accompaniment for smoked salmon.

Medicinal: Antioxidant and thought to be anticarcinogenic but taken in such small amounts that the effect only adds to that of other fruit or vegetables.

> **Note:** Nasturtium seeds (*Tropaeolum species*) and Juniper berries (*Thuja*) can be used in place of capers. Nasturtium seeds have a sharper, more mustard-like flavor.

Couscous

A traditional food of the Maghreb, couscous is a processed flour product or pasta, made by rolling moistened semolina wheat. Tiny granules are formed from the wheat paste by pinching off bits and rolling them to a small oval shape. To keep the small granules separate, they are dusted with finely ground wheat flour. Moroccans use a metal pan similar to a double boiler, called a *couscoussière*, to soften and cook couscous over a steaming, slow-cooking tagine. Traditional couscous may be steamed in a cheesecloth-lined colander placed above a long-cooking soup or stew if a *couscoussière* is not available.

The quick-cooking couscous available in North American food stores is simply soaked in hot, boiled water for a short period of time, fluffed and combined with spices or served plain.

Dates *Phoenix dactylifera*

The fruit of the date palm plant, dates grow in clusters suspended under the leaves. Dates are one of the oldest cultivated tree crops. Dried dates are widely available and keep in a cool dark place for a couple of months. Fresh dates may be found in Middle Eastern markets when in season.

Taste: Sweet and earthy, each variety has a distinct flavor, ranging from strong to delicate.

Culinary: Fresh or dried dates sweeten and add both flavor and fiber to tagine dishes, salads, baked goods, puddings, grain dishes and desserts. Fresh dates are becoming increasingly available and are stuffed whole or chopped into salads and desserts. Date molasses is used in sauces, dips, drinks and dressings.

Medicinal: Laxative; boost estrogen levels; help prevent calcium loss; and are good sources of vitamins A, B_1 (thiamin), B_2 (riboflavin), C and D as well as a valuable source of fiber.

Figs *Ficus carica*

Figs grow on trees that are related to the Mulberry tree. They have been proved to predate the domestication of wheat, barley and legumes. Although used as and considered to be a fruit, figs are actually flowers that grow in groups and are surrounded by pulp. There are over 700 varieties of figs, and they range in color from green to purple or dark brown and black.

Taste: Sweet with delicate floral overtones.

Culinary: Dried figs are readily available in supermarkets throughout the year. In summer and early fall, some supermarkets and most Middle Eastern food markets carry fresh figs. Choose soft, plump fresh figs with thin skins that yield to a gentle touch. Fresh figs contain 12 per cent sugar and are best eaten whole with cheese or other fruit. Cook with dried figs, which contain about 50 per cent sugar. Figs can be substituted for apricots and dates in most tagine recipes.

Medicinal: Figs contain benzaldehyde, a cancer-fighting agent. They are also high in potassium, B vitamins, calcium and magnesium. They are antibacterial, anticancer, antiulcer, digestive, demulcent and laxative.

Legumes

With their high quality plant proteins, leguminous plants, those that grow their seeds in pods, such as peas, beans and lentils, are important to the Mediterranean and Maghreb cuisines. Lentils, fava or broad beans, chickpeas and other legumes are used in tagine dishes, salads, dips and spreads throughout the region.

Culinary: Whole or natural food stores and Middle Eastern, Indian and Caribbean food stores carry a wide selection of dried legumes, both prepackaged and in bulk. All dried legumes except lentils are soaked before they are cooked, in a large pot of water overnight or rehydrated by the quick-soak method.

To quick-soak legumes, bring dried legumes to a boil in a large pot of water over high heat. Reduce heat and simmer for 2 minutes. Remove from the heat and let soak for 1 hour or as long as 12 hours.

To cook soaked legumes (and non-soaked lentils), drain and rinse them and return to the soaking pot. Cover with 2 inches (5 cm) of water and bring to a boil over high heat. Reduce heat and simmer for 15 minutes to 2 hours until tender. Cooking times vary for the different varieties of legumes, with lentils taking the least amount of time to cook. Lentils are cooked when they are soft and easily mashed with a fork.

Medicinal: The high levels of fiber in legumes work to lower cholesterol in the body, protect the colon against cancer and prevent blood sugar levels from rising too rapidly after a meal. They help to control weight by retaining water in the digestive tract, which gives the feeling of fullness. Legumes are high in plant proteins, B vitamins and are a good source of iron, the trace mineral molybdenum (detoxifies sulfites in the body) and choline (improves mental functioning). Legumes also contain vitamins A and C and potassium as well as calcium.

Lemons

Lemon, lime and orange trees grow abundantly in North Africa, and the cuisine takes full advantage of them. Preserved lemons (page 48) perhaps the most popular, have been transformed by salt from their fresh state into a soft and sour-bitter tasting ingredient.

Culinary: Tagine dishes with fish and chicken feature preserved lemons frequently. Dried lime rind gives a hint of citrus when used judiciously in tagines; and orange flower water, like rose water, gives a floral spike to delicate dishes like eggs, puddings and other desserts.

Medicinal: Antioxidant, anticancer; high in vitamin C and limonene, which is thought to inhibit breast cancer.

Nuts

Almonds, walnuts and pistachio nuts are used widely in Moroccan cooking and especially in tagines and pastilla, a meat pie consisting of phyllo dough layered with a mixture of shredded chicken, toasted ground almonds, cinnamon and sugar.

Culinary: Nuts are often toasted to enhance their flavor. To toast nuts, spread out in one layer in the bottom of a tagine dish (or on a rimmed baking sheet). Toast over medium heat, stirring frequently, for 3 minutes (or bake for 3 minutes on the top shelf of a preheated 375°F/190°C oven. Using a metal lifter, turn the nuts over and toast for 1 to 3 minutes, watching closely). Nuts are done when they color slightly. Tip from the dish or baking sheet into a bowl or shallow dish to cool.

Medicinal: Nuts supply protein, vitamin E and fiber along with essential nutrients. Studies have shown that eating nuts is linked to a lower risk for heart disease. This is likely due to their monounsaturated fats and the antioxidant action of the vitamin E. Their linoleic and alpha-linolenic acids are associated with decreased risk of tumor formation and heart disease and are also essential for healthy skin, hair, glands, mucus membranes, nerves and arteries.

Olives

Both olives — fresh, pickled and marinated — and olive oil are essential ingredients in the kitchens of the Maghreb. The markets are the best sources of every kind of olive and every method of preserving them. In fact, the high level of consumption of olive oil is linked to a reduction in coronary heart disease risk. Now avocado oil is replacing olive oil for cooking because it does not lose healing properties when heated (as does olive oil).

Culinary: Used in everyday cooking, olive oil is also used as a dipping sauce with bread in place of butter.

Medicinal: There is evidence that the antioxidants in olive oil improve cholesterol regulation and LDL cholesterol reduction, and that it has other anti-inflammatory and anti-hypertensive effects.

Pomegranate *Punica granatum*

Native to the area, pomegranate is one of the fruits (there are several theories as to the specific fruit), said to have been the forbidden fruit of Adam and Eve. It is certainly an ancient fruit that is rich in the folklore of ancient Persia, India and Southeast Asia. The name is derived from the Latin *pomum* (apple) and *granatus* (seeded) and the Moorish city of Granada in Spain may in fact be named after the fruit.

Culinary: The juicy flesh surrounding the individual seeds has a sweet, slightly astringent flavor and is easily used with either sweet or savory dishes. In addition to using the seeds or ariels fresh, they are also dried and pounded to a powder for seasoning dips, tagines and desserts. Pomegranate Molasses (page 172) is used as a tart spike in tagine dishes, drinks, sauces and dips.

Medicinal: Antidiarrheal; antifever; astringent; used in gargles; thought to reduce fevers and used in Ayurvedic remedies.

Smen (aged butter)

Traditional North African and Middle Eastern cooks use a strongly flavored, goat or sheep milk butter made by heating, salting and aging it. The resulting butter, sometimes years old, is used in traditional dishes and celebratory feasts. Smen (also called sman, semneh or sminn) may be substituted with ghee. While ghee has the same cooking characteristics of smen, it has none of the rancid odor and strong taste of this unique and culturally significant ingredient.

Flavor Combinations

Anise Seasoning

Makes ⅓ cup (75 mL)

Use this delicate seasoning as a rub for fish or chicken or combine with Pernod for a marinade for chicken or fish.

● **Small tagine**

4 tbsp	fennel seeds	60 mL
2 tbsp	coriander seeds	30 mL
2 tsp	cumin seeds	10 mL
1	star anise	1
1	piece (1 inch/2.5 cm) cinnamon, crushed	1
1 tsp	sea salt	5 mL

1. In the bottom of a small tagine, spice wok or skillet, combine fennel, coriander, cumin, star anise and cinnamon. Toast over medium heat, stirring occasionally, for 3 to 4 minutes or until lightly colored and fragrant. Remove from direct heat just as the seeds pop; do not let the spices smoke and burn. Let cool.

2. In a mortar (using pestle) or small electric grinder, pound or grind toasted spices until coarse or finely ground. Stir in sea salt.

3. Store in an airtight (preferably dark) glass jar with lid in a cool place for up to 3 months.

Bahrat Spice Blend

Makes ¼ cup (60 mL)

A general word for "spices," Bahrat may be used to designate several spice blends.

Caution: Purchase sumac from specialist grocery stores selling Middle Eastern ingredients. Some members of the sumac family (found mostly in North America) have poisonous berries.

● **Small tagine**

2 tbsp	coriander seeds	30 mL
4 tsp	cumin seeds	20 mL
1	piece (1 inch/2.5 cm) cinnamon, crushed	1
5	whole cloves	5
½ tsp	cardamom seeds	2 mL
2 tbsp	paprika	30 mL
1 tsp	ground sumac, optional (see Caution, left)	5 mL
½ tsp	ground nutmeg	2 mL

1. In the bottom of a small tagine, spice wok or skillet, combine coriander, cumin, cinnamon, cloves and cardamom. Toast over medium heat, stirring frequently, for 3 to 4 minutes or until lightly colored and fragrant. Remove from direct heat just as the seeds pop; do not let the spices smoke and burn. Let cool.

2. In a mortar (using pestle) or small electric grinder, pound or grind toasted spices until coarse or finely ground. Transfer to a small bowl and stir in paprika, sumac, if using, and nutmeg.

3. Store in an airtight (preferably dark) glass jar with lid in a cool place for up to 3 months.

Chermoula Moroccan Rub

Makes ¾ cup (175 mL)

A marinade/rub for lamb or fish or chicken cooked on the grill.

Tip

Use this rub over meat and let stand in a cool place at least 1 hour before cooking over the grill.

½ cup	coarsely chopped fresh cilantro or flat-leaf parsley	125 mL
¼ cup	sesame seeds	60 mL
2	cloves garlic	2
½ cup	olive oil	125 mL
¼ cup	freshly squeezed lemon juice	60 mL
1 tbsp	paprika	15 mL
1 tsp	hot pepper flakes	5 mL
	Coarse salt	

1. In a food processor or a mortar (using pestle), chop or pound cilantro, sesame seeds and garlic until coarsely ground. With the motor running or by drops, slowly add oil. Blend until smooth.

2. Stir in lemon juice, paprika, hot pepper flakes, and salt to taste. Taste and add more salt or lemon juice if necessary. Use immediately or store in an airtight container in the refrigerator for up to 3 days.

Coriander Pesto

Makes 1¼ cups (300 mL)

Both cilantro (the green leaves) and coriander seeds are parts of the same plant, *Coriandrum sativum.*

● **Food processor or blender**

2	cloves garlic	2
¼ cup	pine nuts	60 mL
1 tbsp	crushed coriander seeds	15 mL
1	fresh green chile pepper, quartered	1
2 cups	fresh cilantro leaves	500 mL
¼ cup	freshly grated Parmesan cheese	60 mL
½ cup	olive oil (approx.)	125 mL
	Salt	

1. In a food processor or blender, process garlic, nuts and coriander seeds for 15 seconds or until chopped. Add chile pepper, cilantro and Parmesan. Process for 30 to 40 seconds or until chopped. With motor running, add olive oil through opening in the lid in a steady stream. Keep adding oil and blending until pesto has reached the desired consistency. Add salt to taste. Process for 3 seconds to blend.

2. Store, tightly covered, in the refrigerator for up to 1 week or in the freezer for up to 3 months.

Berbere

Makes ¼ cup (60 mL)

Called berbere in Ethiopia, this hot and fragrant blend can be used to flavor vegetable tagines or used with legume dishes.

● **Small tagine**

5	dried cayenne peppers	5
1 tbsp	black peppercorns	15 mL
2 tsp	allspice berries	10 mL
1 tsp	cumin seeds	5 mL
1 tsp	cardamom seeds	5 mL
1 tsp	fenugreek seeds	5 mL
3	whole cloves	3
1	piece (1 inch/2.5 cm) cinnamon, crushed	1

1. Using scissors, cut cayenne pepper pods into small pieces. In the bottom of a small tagine, spice wok or skillet, combine pepper pieces with peppercorns, allspice, cumin, cardamom, fenugreek, cloves and cinnamon. Toast over medium heat, stirring occasionally, for 3 to 4 minutes or until lightly colored and fragrant. Remove from direct heat just as the seeds pop; do not let the spices smoke and burn. Let cool.

2. In a mortar (using pestle) or small electric grinder, pound or grind toasted spices until coarse or finely ground.

3. Store in an airtight (preferably dark) glass jar with lid in a cool place for up to 3 months.

Fennel Seasoning

Makes ⅓ cup (75 mL)

I often add 2 tbsp (30 mL) of dried fennel leaf that I have saved from times when I cook with fresh fennel bulb, but this is not readily available unless you dry it yourself.

● **Small tagine**

2 tbsp	fennel seeds	30 mL
1 tbsp	coriander seeds	15 mL
2 tsp	cumin seeds	10 mL
1 tsp	cardamom seeds	5 mL
1 tsp	fenugreek seeds	5 mL
2	whole cloves	2
1	piece (1 inch/2.5 cm) cinnamon, crushed	1
1 tsp	sea salt	5 mL

1. In the bottom of a small tagine, spice wok or skillet, combine fennel, coriander, cumin, cardamom, fenugreek, cloves and cinnamon. Toast over medium heat, stirring frequently, for 3 to 4 minutes or until lightly colored and fragrant. Remove from direct heat just as the seeds pop; do not let the spices smoke and burn. Let cool.

2. In a mortar (using pestle) or small electric grinder, pound or grind toasted spices until coarse or finely ground. Stir in sea salt.

3. Store in an airtight (preferably dark) glass jar with lid in a cool place for up to 3 months.

Ground Moroccan Spice Blend

Makes ½ cup (125 mL)

I make this quick and easy spice blend when I don't have time to roast and grind a whole spice blend.

3 tbsp	ground cinnamon	45 mL
2 tbsp	ground cardamom	30 mL
2 tbsp	ground coriander	30 mL
1 tbsp	ground cumin	15 mL
1 tsp	ground cloves	5 mL
1 tsp	ground ginger	5 mL

1. In a bowl, combine cinnamon, cardamom, coriander, cumin, cloves and ginger. Store in an airtight (preferably dark) glass jar with lid in a cool place for up to 3 months.

La Kama Spice Blend

Makes 3 tbsp (45 mL)

A light yet fragrant spice blend, my version does not toast the spices before grinding them. La Kama is often used in harira, the lentil and tomato soup eaten to break the Ramadan fast. It's an all-round mixture that serves as a seasoning for both meat and meatless tagine dishes.

1 tbsp	black or green peppercorns	15 mL
2 tsp	cumin seeds	10 mL
2	whole cloves	2
2 tsp	ground turmeric	10 mL
1 tbsp	minced fresh gingerroot	15 mL
½ tsp	ground nutmeg	2 mL

1. In a mortar (using pestle) or small electric grinder, combine peppercorns, cumin, cloves and turmeric. Pound or grind spices until finely ground. Add ginger and nutmeg and mix well. Use immediately or store in an airtight container in the refrigerator for up to 3 days.

Harissa

Makes ½ cup (125 mL)

Widely used in Morocco, Tunisia and Algeria, harissa is a fiery sauce used almost in the same way that North Americans use ketchup. It is passed separately as a dip for grilled meat or couscous, stirred into soups and stews, or added to other dips. If stirred into yogurt, it serves as a hot marinade for lamb and chicken.

Variation

For a less pungent sauce, use 6 chiles instead of the 12 called for above. Add 2 skinned roasted red bell peppers in Step 4 with the soaked chiles.

● **Small tagine**

12	dried red chile peppers	12
¾ cup	boiling water	175 mL
1 tbsp	coriander seeds	15 mL
2 tsp	cumin seeds	10 mL
1 tsp	fennel seeds	5 mL
½ tsp	fenugreek seeds, optional	2 mL
2	cloves garlic	2
½ tsp	sea salt	2 mL
½ cup	avocado or olive oil	125 mL

1. Discard stems from chiles. Over a bowl, cut chiles into strips using kitchen scissors. Pour water over. Let soak for about 30 minutes or until softened. Drain.

2. Meanwhile, in the bottom of a small tagine, spice wok or skillet, combine coriander, cumin, fennel and fenugreek. Toast over medium heat, stirring frequently, for 3 to 4 minutes or until lightly colored and fragrant. Remove from direct heat just as the seeds pop; do not let the spices smoke and burn. Let cool.

3. In a mortar (using pestle) or small electric grinder, pound or grind toasted spices until finely ground. Transfer to a separate bowl.

4. In same mortar (using pestle) or a food processor, pound or chop garlic with salt. Add drained chiles and pound or process until smooth. Add toasted spices. If using a mortar, gradually pound in oil, trickling it in and mixing with all ingredients. If using a food processor, with motor running, add oil in a steady stream through opening in feed tube. The sauce should be smooth and well blended with a mayonnaise-like consistency, but will be coarser if made in a mortar by hand. Use immediately or store in an airtight container in the refrigerator for up to 3 weeks.

Mediterranean Pesto

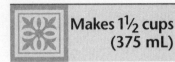

Makes 1½ cups (375 mL)

With all the flavors of the Mediterranean, this pesto is a natural when teamed with roasted red peppers or other dishes from the Mediterranean region.

● **Food processor or blender**

2	cloves garlic	2
2	slices candied ginger	2
½ cup	natural almonds	125 mL
1 cup	fresh basil leaves	250 mL
½ cup	fresh thyme leaves	125 mL
½ cup	fresh savory or oregano leaves	125 mL
2 tbsp	fresh rosemary leaves, optional	30 mL
¼ cup	freshly grated Parmesan cheese	60 mL
½ cup	olive oil (approx.)	125 mL
	Salt	

1. In a food processor or blender, process garlic, ginger and almonds for 20 seconds or until minced. Add basil, thyme, savory, rosemary, if using, and sprinkle Parmesan over herbs. Process for 30 to 40 seconds or until chopped. With motor running, add olive oil through opening in the lid in a steady stream until well blended. Keep adding oil and blending until pesto has reached the desired consistency. Add salt to taste. Process for 3 seconds to blend.

2. Store, tightly covered, in the refrigerator for up to 1 week or in the freezer for up to 2 months.

Moroccan Cinnamon Spice Blend

Makes ¼ cup (60 mL)

Very aromatic without being overpoweringly hot, this spice blend is versatile for tagine dishes that include fruit and can even be used in small amounts in sweet dishes and beverages.

● **Small tagine**

1	piece (2 inches/5 cm) cinnamon, crushed	1
2 tbsp	cardamom seeds	30 mL
2 tbsp	coriander seeds	30 mL
1 tbsp	cumin seeds	15 mL
2 tsp	black peppercorns	10 mL
3	whole cloves	3
1	star anise	1
¼ tsp	ground nutmeg	1 mL

1. In the bottom of a small tagine, spice wok or skillet, combine cinnamon, cardamom, coriander, cumin, peppercorns, cloves and star anise. Toast over medium-high heat, stirring occasionally, for 4 to 5 minutes or until lightly colored and fragrant. Remove from direct heat just as the seeds pop; do not let the spices smoke and burn. Let cool.

2. In a mortar (using pestle) or small electric grinder, pound or grind toasted spices until coarse or finely ground. Add nutmeg to ground spices and mix well.

3. Store in an airtight (preferably dark) glass jar with lid in a cool place for up to 3 months.

Preserved Lemons

Makes 9 preserved lemons

When I can get the small Meyer or Sudachi lemons, I always preserve some of them using this simple recipe. When my stash of preserved lemons runs out, I toss half a dozen fresh lemons into the freezer (page 49) and use them as a quick substitution for the traditional salt preserved lemons.

● **1 large wide-mouth jar with lid, sterilized**

12 to 14	small, thin-skinned organic lemons	12 to 14
	Kosher or table salt	

1. Scrub lemons. Squeeze juice from 3 lemons, reserving juice and discarding rinds.

2. Working on a cutting surface, remove and discard the bottom and top from 9 of the remaining lemons. Set one lemon on end and make a vertical cut from the top, three-quarters of the way toward the bottom, so the two halves remain attached at the base, being careful not to cut the lemon in half. Turn the lemon upside down so the base is now at the top. Rotate it and make a second vertical cut down the center from the top, at cross-angles to the first cut, leaving the bottom attached.

3. Working over a bowl, fill the slits with as much salt as the lemon will hold and place in jar. Repeat with 4 of the remaining lemons. Pour reserved lemon juice over lemons in the jar and push down with a spoon to compact them. Slit and fill the 4 remaining trimmed lemons and push into the jar. Lemons should be immersed in juice and if not, squeeze remaining 2 lemons if necessary and add to jar to cover salted lemons.

4. Secure the lid and set the jar aside at cool room temperature for 6 weeks, shaking it from time to time.

5. Store in refrigerator for up to 6 months after opening.

> **To use Preserved Lemons:** Rinse well and remove the soft, jam-like flesh. Cut the rind into thin strips or chop fine and add to cooked tagine dishes in the final 15 minutes of the cooking time. The flesh may be added to a tagine sauce or not, according to preference.

Frozen Lemons

**Makes 6
frozen lemons**

Frozen lemons release more juice than fresh and the rind is softened and milder in taste than either preserved or fresh lemons. Although I make a batch of traditionally preserved lemons about once a year (page 48), I always have a bag of lemons in the freezer. I use all parts of frozen lemons: the rind, the juice and the pulp in some tagine recipes.

- **Medium resealable freezer bag**

| 6 | organic lemons | 6 |

1. Scrub lemons. Place in resealable freezer bag and freeze for up to 4 months.

To use Frozen Lemons: One frozen lemon takes about 1 hour to thaw but it is not necessary to completely thaw before using. Run hot water from a tap over a frozen lemon for 30 seconds to a minute or just until it is soft enough to cut in half. You can then squeeze or chop flesh and/or rind while still frozen.

Ras el Hanout

Makes ⅓ cup (75 mL)

In Morocco, every stall in the *attarine* (spice street in the market) has its own ras el hanout. The literal meaning is "top of the shop" and it is the very best the spice merchant has to offer. This is a secret blend of upwards of 25, sometimes 100 different spices, herbs, and aphrodisiacs that people search out until they find the one they love best. A mortar and pestle works best to crush and grind the toasted spices, but if necessary, use a spice grinder or small food processor.

Variation

Just before adding to a dish, add one minced garlic clove and ¼ tsp (1 mL) finely shredded fresh gingerroot for every 1 to 2 tbsp (15 to 30 mL) Ras el Hanout blend.

● **Small tagine**

1 tbsp	allspice berries	15 mL
1 tbsp	coriander seeds	15 mL
1 tbsp	fennel seeds	15 mL
1	piece (2 inches/5 cm) cinnamon, crushed	1
2 tsp	cardamom seeds	10 mL
2 tsp	cumin seeds	10 mL
2 tsp	fenugreek seeds	10 mL
2 tsp	black peppercorns	10 mL
3	cloves	3
1	star anise	1
1 tbsp	sea salt	15 mL
1 tbsp	ground turmeric	15 mL
1 tsp	ground ginger	5 mL

1. In the bottom of a small tagine, spice wok or skillet, combine allspice, coriander, fennel, cinnamon, cardamom, cumin, fenugreek, peppercorns, cloves and star anise. Toast over medium heat, stirring frequently, for 3 to 4 minutes or until lightly colored and fragrant. Remove from direct heat just as the seeds pop; do not let the spices smoke and burn. Let cool.

2. In a mortar (using pestle) or small electric grinder, pound or grind toasted spices until coarse or finely ground. Transfer to a small bowl and stir in salt, turmeric and ginger.

3. Store in an airtight (preferably dark) glass jar with lid in a cool place for up to 3 months.

Roasted Red Peppers

Makes 2 cups (500 mL)

Either fresh hot chile peppers or sweet red bell peppers may be roasted, but for most of the recipes in this book, it is the sweet variety that is used. Roasted peppers take time to make in quantity but with many hands the whole process becomes a social event — an autumn tradition.

Tips

For Step 1, char peppers over barbecue flame instead of in the oven.

To make large quantities, multiply the recipe ingredients by up to 10. Freeze in 2-cup (500 mL) quantities in freezer bags for up to 3 months.

● **Preheat broiler, position oven rack on top rung**

4	red bell peppers, halved and seeded	4
1/3 cup	olive oil	75 mL
3 tbsp	balsamic vinegar	45 mL
6	large basil leaves, thinly sliced crosswise	6
4	cloves garlic, thinly sliced lengthwise	4

1. Place bell pepper halves cut side down on a baking sheet. Broil in preheated oven on top rack directly under heat, turning pan often, for 5 to 8 minutes, until skin is evenly charred.

2. Meanwhile, in a bowl, whisk together oil, vinegar, basil and garlic. Set aside.

3. Remove blackened peppers from oven. Set baking sheet on a cooling rack and cover peppers with a clean towel. Let cool. Remove the charred skins from peppers. They should slip off easily when rubbed. Slice pepper halves into 1/2-inch (1 cm) wide strips and place in bowl with oil mixture. Toss pepper slices to coat evenly. Cover dish tightly with plastic wrap and marinate for at least 2 hours at room temperature or for up to 3 days in the refrigerator.

Taklia Spice Blend

Makes ¼ cup (60 mL)

Use this simple Egyptian blend in soups and stews, dressings or sauces.

● Small tagine

3	cloves garlic	3
1½ tsp	sea salt	7 mL
2 tbsp	avocado or olive oil	30 mL
2 tsp	ground coriander	10 mL
½ tsp	cayenne powder	2 mL

1. In a mortar (using pestle), crush garlic with salt. In bottom of a small tagine or a small, heavy-bottomed pan, heat oil over medium heat. Add garlic and salt and cook, stirring, for 2 to 3 minutes, until golden. Stir in coriander and cayenne powder and mix to a paste. Cook, stirring constantly, for 2 minutes. Use immediately or store in an airtight container in the refrigerator for up to 5 days.

Tamarind Water

Makes ½ cup (125 mL)

Often used in Middle Eastern recipes, tamarind water is easy to prepare and may be made in larger quantities in advance, and frozen in ice cube trays. When used with sugar, it imparts a sweet-sour flavor.

½ cup	boiling water	125 mL
1	walnut-size piece tamarind pulp, about 1-inch (2.5 cm) square	1

1. In a small bowl, pour water over tamarind. Let stand for 20 minutes. Strain through a fine mesh sieve over a bowl or measuring cup, pressing pulp and squeezing solids dry. Discard solids. Use immediately or store in an airtight container in the refrigerator for up to 2 days or freeze in 1 tbsp (15 mL) portions in ice cube trays.

Tabil Spice Blend

Makes ¼ cup (60 mL)

Tabil is the word for coriander and it may be used to define any spice blend similar to this. Use with meat or vegetable tagine recipes.

- **Preheat oven to 250°F (130°C)**

3 tbsp	coriander seeds	45 mL
1 tbsp	caraway seeds	15 mL
2	cloves garlic, chopped	2
2 tsp	hot paprika or chili powder	10 mL

1. In a small bowl, combine coriander, caraway, garlic and paprika. Spread on a baking sheet and dry in preheated oven for 30 to 45 minutes. Let cool. Grind in a mortar (using a pestle) or spice grinder.

2. Store in an airtight (preferably dark) glass jar with lid in a cool place for up to 3 months.

Turmeric Spice Paste

Makes ¼ cup (60 mL)

Pastes are easy to use in cooking because they blend easily into dishes as they simmer. Make small amounts and always store spice pastes in the refrigerator. Fresh turmeric is not always available and when it is, it is usually only found in Indian spice specialty stores. This recipe may be made in a blender, but a mortar and pestle works best.

Variation

Use 2 tbsp (30 mL) ground turmeric in place of the fresh and add in Step 2.

- **Small tagine**

1	piece (1 inch/2.5 cm) cinnamon, crushed	1
1 tbsp	coriander seeds	15 mL
1 tbsp	allspice berries	15 mL
1	whole clove	1
1	piece (2 inches/5 cm) fresh turmeric root	1
1	piece (½ inch/1 cm) fresh gingerroot	1
2	cloves garlic	2
2 tbsp	olive oil (approx.)	30 mL

1. In the bottom of a small tagine, spice wok or skillet, combine cinnamon, coriander, allspice and clove. Toast over medium-high heat, stirring occasionally, for 3 to 4 minutes or until lightly colored and fragrant. Remove from direct heat just as the seeds pop; do not let the spices smoke and burn. Let cool.

2. In a mortar (using pestle), pound toasted spices until finely ground. Add turmeric, ginger and garlic. Pound, stopping to add oil every few seconds until a smooth paste is formed. Use immediately or store in an airtight container in the refrigerator for up to 1 week or in the freezer for up to 2 months.

Tunisian Five Spices

Makes 3 tbsp (45 mL)

Similar to the Chinese five-spice blend, this mixture is rich in flavor.

● **Small tagine**

1 tbsp	coriander seeds	15 mL
1 tbsp	whole cloves	15 mL
2 tsp	green or black peppercorns	10 mL
1	piece (1 inch/2.5 cm) cinnamon, crushed	1
1 tbsp	ground nutmeg	15 mL

1. In the bottom of a small tagine, spice wok or skillet, combine coriander, cloves, peppercorns and cinnamon. Toast over medium heat, stirring frequently, for 2 to 3 minutes or until lightly colored and fragrant. Remove from direct heat just as the seeds pop; do not let the spices smoke and burn. Let cool.

2. In a mortar (using pestle) or small electric grinder, pound or grind toasted spices until coarse or finely ground. Transfer to a small bowl and stir in nutmeg.

3. Store in an airtight (preferably dark) glass jar with lid in a cool place for up to 3 months.

Za'atar

Makes ¼ cup (60 mL)

Za'atar is a term used for a blend of spices that have an overall aroma of thyme or oregano. Use as a rub for fish or sprinkle over oiled flat bread and toast for a tasty snack.

2 tbsp	toasted sesame seeds	30 mL
1 tbsp	dried thyme	15 mL
2 tsp	ground sumac or paprika (see Caution, below)	10 mL
2 tsp	dried oregano	10 mL
1 tsp	sea salt	5 mL

1. In a small dark glass jar, combine sesame seeds, thyme, sumac, oregano and salt. Cover with lid and shake to mix well. Label and store in a cool place for up to 2 months.

Caution: Purchase sumac from specialist grocery stores selling Middle Eastern ingredients. Some members of the sumac family (found mostly in North America) have poisonous berries.

Poultry

Buttered Turmeric Chicken Tagine

Makes 4 to 6 servings

The ground turmeric gives the chicken and vegetables a yellow glow. This is a hearty tagine and all that is needed to complete the meal is plain couscous or rice.

- Medium or large tagine
- Baking sheet, lined with parchment or waxed paper

1 tbsp	ground turmeric	15 mL
1 tbsp	ground cumin	15 mL
1 tsp	ground sea salt	5 mL
6	skinless bone-in chicken thighs (about 2 lbs/1 kg)	6
2 tbsp	avocado or olive oil (see Tip, right)	30 mL
2 tbsp	butter, divided	30 mL
2	onions, cut into quarters	2
1 tbsp	Ras el Hanout (page 50) or store-bought	15 mL
4	cloves garlic, coarsely chopped	4
1 tbsp	crushed coriander seeds	15 mL
6	fresh turnips, cut in half	6
½ cup	chopped dried apricots	125 mL
1	can (14 to 19 oz/398 to 540 mL) chickpeas, drained and rinsed	1

1. In a large bowl, combine turmeric, cumin and salt. Place chicken thighs, meaty side up, on prepared baking sheet. Sprinkle turmeric mixture evenly over chicken and rub seasoning into the flesh. Cover tightly and set aside in refrigerator for 30 minutes or as long as overnight. Let meat return to room temperature before cooking.

2. In the bottom of a flameproof tagine, heat oil and melt 1 tbsp (15 mL) of the butter over medium heat. Add onions and ras el hanout and cook, stirring, for 5 minutes. Add garlic and coriander and cook, stirring, for 2 minutes. Add chicken, meaty side down, sliding thighs around and moving vegetables away from bottom so that flesh is in direct contact with bottom of tagine. Cook for 4 to 5 minutes or until chicken is browned on meaty side.

I recommend the use of organic, cold-pressed extra virgin avocado oil in the tagine recipes in this book because it is excellent for medium to high heat cooking. Unlike other polyunsaturated oils, olive oil in particular, avocado oil does not break down under high heat cooking. It is an excellent source of vitamin E and contains beneficial omega-3, 6 and 9 fatty acids.

3. Using tongs, turn chicken over. Add remaining butter and turnips, stirring, until butter is melted. Cover with tagine lid, reduce heat to low and simmer for 25 minutes without lifting the lid.

4. Stir in apricots and chickpeas. Replace lid and simmer for 10 to 15 minutes or until apricots are plump, chickpeas are heated through, vegetables are tender and juices run clear when chicken is pierced with a fork.

Chicken and Vegetables with Raisins and Olives

Makes 4 to 6 servings

The sweetness of the raisins is balanced by the olives and preserved lemon in this tasty tagine.

Tip

I make this tagine at the end of my growing season and use small green tomatoes, but you can use hothouse cherry tomatoes or 1 can (14 oz/398 mL) drained plum tomatoes.

● **Medium or large tagine**

3 tbsp	avocado or olive oil	45 mL
2	onions, cut into quarters	2
1 tbsp	Ras el Hanout (page 50) or store-bought	15 mL
6	cloves garlic, sliced	6
12	cherry tomatoes, cut in half (see Tip, left)	12
1 tsp	hot pepper flakes, optional	5 mL
6	skinless bone-in chicken thighs (about 2 lbs/1 kg)	6
	Juice of 1 fresh lemon	
	Flesh and rind of ½ Preserved Lemon (page 48), chopped, optional	
3 cups	shredded cabbage	750 mL
2 cups	diced turnip	500 mL
½ cup	raisins	125 mL

1. In the bottom of a flameproof tagine, heat oil over medium heat. Add onions and ras el hanout and cook, stirring, for 5 minutes. Add garlic, tomatoes and hot pepper flakes and cook, stirring, for 2 minutes. Add chicken, meaty side down, sliding breasts around and moving vegetables away from bottom so that flesh is in direct contact with bottom of tagine. Cook for about 5 minutes or until chicken is browned on meaty side.

2. Using tongs, turn chicken over. Add lemon juice and chopped lemon rind and flesh, if using. Add cabbage and turnip to tagine. Cover with tagine lid, reduce heat to low and simmer, stirring once, for 25 minutes.

3. Stir in raisins. Replace lid and simmer for 10 to 15 minutes or until raisins are plump, vegetables are tender and juices run clear when chicken is pierced with a fork.

Chicken Meatballs with Spiced Lentils and Squash

Makes 4 servings

I have found that there are some very good store-bought frozen meatballs available with very little fat and sodium and no preservatives. Check labels and try different brands to find one that you like because they save time in dishes like this easy weeknight tagine. Baking the meatballs in the oven makes them crisp on the outside so they do not break down when added to the tagine.

Tip

You don't have to buy meatballs. Try ground chicken, turkey, beef or lamb to make your own homemade meatballs for this dish. See my homemade meatball recipe (page 94).

- **Medium tagine**
- **Preheat oven to 350°F (180°C)**

3 tbsp	avocado or olive oil, divided	45 mL
1	onion, chopped	1
1 tbsp	Moroccan Cinnamon Spice Blend (page 47) or store-bought garam masala	15 mL
2 tsp	ground fenugreek	10 mL
2 tsp	ground turmeric	10 mL
1 tsp	ground ginger	5 mL
1 cup	brown, red, green or yellow lentils, rinsed and drained	250 mL
2 cups	water	500 mL
1	can (28 oz/796 mL) diced tomatoes with juice	1
2 cups	diced squash or pumpkin	500 mL
¼ cup	raisins	60 mL
16	medium uncooked chicken meatballs (see Intro, left)	16

1. In the bottom of a flameproof tagine, heat oil over medium heat. Add onion, spice blend, fenugreek, turmeric and ginger and cook, stirring, for 5 minutes. Add lentils and stir until coated with onions and spices. Add water and bring to a boil. Cover with tagine lid, reduce heat to low and simmer for 25 minutes or until lentils are just tender and not mushy.

2. Add tomatoes with juice and squash. Increase heat to medium and bring to a boil. Replace lid, reduce heat to low and simmer for 15 minutes. Stir in raisins and cook for 10 to 15 minutes or until squash is tender.

3. Meanwhile, bake meatballs in preheated oven for 12 to 15 minutes or according to package directions. Add meatballs to tagine and serve.

Chicken with Caramelized Onions

**Makes
4 servings**

The eggplant and chicken are not browned in this recipe but North African recipe techniques for eggplant often include char grilling them over an open flame. You can grill the eggplant in this recipe in the oven under a broiler for a traditional North African effect if you wish.

Tip

Long, thin Asian varieties of eggplant work well in this recipe but you can use one larger, fat eggplant and cut it into eight wedges lengthwise.

● **Medium tagine**

	Juice of 1 fresh lemon	
20	saffron threads	20
3 tbsp	avocado or olive oil	45 mL
4	onions, sliced	4
1 tsp	ground ginger	5 mL
1 tsp	ground cinnamon	5 mL
½ tsp	ground allspice	2 mL
2 tbsp	liquid honey	30 mL
4	skinless boneless chicken breasts (about 1½ lbs/750 g)	4
2	long thin eggplants (about 1 lb/500 g), cut into quarters (see Tip, left)	2

1. In a small bowl, pour lemon juice over saffron and set aside.

2. In the bottom of a flameproof tagine, heat oil over medium heat. Add onions, ginger, cinnamon and allspice and cook, stirring, for 5 minutes. Reduce heat to low and cook, stirring frequently, for 10 minutes or until onions are soft and light golden. Stir in honey until incorporated. Add chicken, sliding breasts around and moving onions away from bottom so that flesh is in direct contact with bottom of tagine.

3. Add eggplant wedges and pour saffron and lemon juice over all. Bring liquids to a boil over medium heat. Cover with tagine lid, reduce heat to low and simmer, stirring once, for 30 to 40 minutes or until chicken is no longer pink inside.

Chicken with Dried Fruit and Peppers

Makes 4 to 6 servings

The dried fruit sweetens the tagine and if you serve preserved or fresh lemon wedges with it, the dish is balanced with tart, spicy and sweet flavors.

● **Medium or large tagine**

3 tbsp	avocado or olive oil	45 mL
3	onions, cut into quarters	3
1 tbsp	Ras el Hanout (page 50) or store-bought	15 mL
6	skinless bone-in chicken thighs (about 2 lbs/1 kg)	6
3	red bell peppers, cut into eighths	3
15	dried apricots, cut in half	15
15	pitted prunes, cut in half	15
¼ cup	chopped dried figs	60 mL
3 tbsp	chopped dates	45 mL
½ cup	chicken broth or water	125 mL
4 to 6	Preserved Lemons (page 48) or fresh lemon wedges	4 to 6

1. In the bottom of a flameproof tagine, heat oil over medium heat. Add onions and ras el hanout and cook, stirring, for 5 minutes. Add chicken, meaty side down, sliding thighs around and moving onions away from bottom so that flesh is in direct contact with bottom of tagine. Cook for about 5 minutes or until chicken is browned on meaty side.

2. Using tongs, turn chicken over. Add bell peppers, apricots, prunes, figs and dates. Pour broth over and bring to a boil. Cover with tagine lid, reduce heat to low and simmer, stirring once, for 25 to 30 minutes or until juices run clear when chicken is pierced with a fork.

Chicken with Persian Sauce

Makes 4 servings

The sauce for this dish is rich and exotic and it is thickened by reduction, a different technique for the tagine. You can use duck in place of the chicken breasts for a dramatic dish. Serve chicken and the fruity sauce over rice or couscous with a salad or cooked vegetables.

Tip

If you can't find ras el hanout, garam masala is a fine substitute.

Variation

Duck with Persian Sauce: The use of duck in North African tagines is likely a modern throwback from the French influence when their rule extended across most of North Africa and about one-third of the northwestern regions. If you wish to use duck in this (or any of the chicken) recipes, it will be rich and tender and you may find that the orange juice could be reduced by about 1/4 cup (60 mL).

● **Medium tagine**

3 tbsp	avocado or olive oil	45 mL
2	onions, cut in half and thinly sliced	2
1 tbsp	Ras el Hanout (page 50) or store-bought (see Tip, left)	15 mL
1 cup	freshly squeezed orange juice	250 mL
1/2 cup	chicken broth	125 mL
	Juice of 1 fresh lemon	
1 cup	coarsely chopped walnuts	250 mL
1/2 cup	chopped dried cherries	125 mL
3 tbsp	liquid honey	45 mL
4	skinless boneless chicken breasts (about 2 lbs/1 kg)	4

1. In the bottom of a flameproof tagine, heat oil over medium heat. Add onions and ras el hanout and cook, stirring, for 10 to 15 minutes or until onions are soft. Add orange juice, chicken broth and lemon juice. Bring to a boil and boil gently for about 20 minutes, adjusting the heat to keep the mixture gently boiling. Liquids should be slightly thickened and reduced in volume by roughly one-quarter.

2. Stir in walnuts, cherries, honey and chicken. Bring to a boil, cover with tagine lid, reduce heat to low and simmer, stirring once, for 30 to 40 minutes or until chicken is no longer pink inside.

Cinnamon Chicken Tagine with Peaches

Makes 4 servings

Having canned peaches or apricots on hand for this dish makes sense when busy schedules prevent lengthy preparation. This is an easy and delicious dish for a weekday dinner.

● **Medium tagine**

2 tbsp	avocado or olive oil	30 mL
1	onion, cut into quarters	1
2 tsp	Ground Moroccan Spice Blend (page 44) or ground cinnamon	10 mL
1 tsp	ground ginger	5 mL
1 tsp	hot pepper flakes, optional	5 mL
4	skinless boneless chicken breasts (about 1½ lbs/750 g)	4
	Juice of 1 fresh lemon	
1	can (14 oz/398 mL) sliced peaches or apricots in water or juice	1
2 cups	carrot coins	500 mL
¼ cup	toasted slivered almonds	60 mL

1. In the bottom of a flameproof tagine, heat oil over medium heat. Add onion, spice blend, ginger and hot pepper flakes, if using and cook, stirring, for 5 minutes. Add chicken and toss with onion and spices to coat.

2. Add lemon juice, peaches and liquid and carrots. Bring to a boil, cover with tagine lid, reduce heat to low and simmer, stirring once, for 30 to 40 minutes or until chicken is no longer pink inside. Garnish with almonds.

Citrus Chicken Tagine

**Makes
4 servings**

Poultry cooked with dates and honey is an ancient Middle Eastern dish, and North Africans use chicken, duck or pigeon in similar tagine combinations. The skin is left on the chicken for this dish and it cooks with little moisture.

Tip

Whole, succulent Medjool dates from California are available in many food stores from the fall throughout the early winter and they are perfect in this tagine, but if you can find other varieties such as Bahri, Hayani, Deglet Noor or Khalas, they will be just as good.

● **Medium tagine**

1	piece (1 inch/2.5 cm) fresh gingerroot	1
1	piece (1 inch/2.5 cm) fresh turmeric or 1 tbsp (15 mL) ground turmeric	1
3	cloves garlic	3
2 tbsp	avocado or olive oil	30 mL
1 tbsp	butter	15 mL
1	piece (2 inches/5 cm) cinnamon stick, crushed fine	1
1 tbsp	cumin seeds	15 mL
4	bone-in chicken pieces with skin (about 1½ lbs/750 g)	4
1	orange, sectioned	1
½ cup	whole dates (see Tip, left)	125 mL
½ cup	freshly squeezed orange juice or orange flower water	125 mL
2 tbsp	freshly squeezed lemon juice	30 mL
2 tbsp	Pomegranate Molasses (page 172) or store-bought or liquid honey	30 mL
¼ cup	blanched almonds	60 mL

1. In a mortar (using a pestle), smash ginger, turmeric and garlic. Pound and grind until a paste is achieved. Or, using a small food processor, blend ginger, turmeric and garlic into a paste.

2. In the bottom of a flameproof tagine, heat oil and melt butter over medium heat. Add spice paste, cinnamon and cumin and cook, stirring frequently, for 3 to 5 minutes or until paste is lightly colored. Add chicken and toss to coat in the spices. Cook, turning frequently, for about 7 minutes or until chicken is browned on both sides.

3. Using tongs, turn chicken so that the skin is up. Tuck orange sections and dates around chicken. Stir in orange juice, lemon juice and molasses and bring to a boil. Cover with tagine lid, reduce heat to low and simmer for 30 to 40 minutes or until chicken juices run clear for thighs and is no longer pink inside for breasts. Garnish with almonds.

Garlic Lemon Chicken Tagine

 Makes 4 to 6 servings

One of the interesting things about cooking is that it truly is, in some ways, alchemy. Here we incorporate three bulbs of garlic into the ingredients and the taste is deliciously mild. The reason is that the garlic cooks for a very long time, allowing the sulphur components that give garlic its strong taste and aroma to dissipate.

Tip

I recommend the use of organic, cold-pressed extra virgin avocado oil in the tagine recipes in this book because it is excellent for medium to high heat cooking. Unlike other polyunsaturated oils, olive oil in particular, avocado oil does not break down under high heat cooking. It is an excellent source of vitamin E and contains beneficial omega-3, 6 and 9 fatty acids.

- Medium or large tagine
- Baking sheet, lined with parchment or waxed paper

4 to 6	skinless bone-in chicken pieces (about 2½ lbs/1.25 kg)	4 to 6
1	Preserved Lemon or Frozen Lemon (pages 48 and 49), cut in half	1
1 tbsp	Bahrat Spice Blend (page 39) or store-bought garam masala	15 mL
3 tbsp	avocado or olive oil (see Tip, left)	45 mL
2	onions, cut into quarters	2
3	heads garlic, cloves peeled (about 30)	3
¼ cup	chicken broth	60 mL
2 tbsp	liquid honey	30 mL
2 cups	diced squash or rutabaga	500 mL
¼ cup	chopped fresh or dried figs	60 mL

1. Place chicken pieces in one layer, meaty side up, on prepared baking sheet. Rub chicken with one Preserved Lemon half. Sprinkle spice blend evenly over chicken and rub into the flesh. Cover tightly and set aside in refrigerator for 30 minutes or overnight. Let meat return to room temperature before cooking.

2. In the bottom of a flameproof tagine, heat oil over medium heat. Add onions and garlic cloves and cook, stirring, for 5 minutes. Add chicken, meaty side down, sliding pieces around and moving onions away from bottom so that flesh is in direct contact with bottom of tagine. Cook for about 5 minutes or until chicken is browned on meaty side.

3. Meanwhile, juice remaining half of Preserved Lemon and chop rind and flesh. Using tongs, turn chicken over. Add lemon juice and chopped preserved lemon rind and flesh. Stir in broth and honey until incorporated. Spread squash over chicken and bring liquids to a boil, stirring occasionally. Cover with tagine lid, reduce heat to low and simmer, stirring once, for 25 minutes.

4. Stir in figs. Replace lid and simmer for 10 to 15 minutes or until vegetables are tender and chicken is no longer pink inside for breasts and juices run clear for thighs.

Golden Chicken with Potatoes and Chickpeas

Makes 4 to 6 servings

Two colorful and aromatic spices combine in this beautiful dish for tastes fit for a sultan. Chickpeas and potatoes give substance to the tagine, which carries the meal.

Tip

For chicken pieces, you can use breasts, legs, thighs or drumsticks.

● **Medium or large tagine**

3 tbsp	melted butter	45 mL
20	strands saffron	20
1 tbsp	ground turmeric	15 mL
3 tbsp	avocado or olive oil	45 mL
2	onions, cut into quarters	2
4	medium potatoes, cut into wedges	4
4 to 6	skinless bone-in chicken pieces (about 2½ lbs/1.25 kg) (see Tip, left)	4 to 6
1 cup	chicken broth	250 mL
1	piece (2 inches/5 cm) cinnamon stick	1
1	can (14 to 19 oz/398 to 540 mL) chickpeas, drained and rinsed	1
¼ cup	chopped flat-leaf parsley	60 mL

1. In a bowl, combine melted butter, saffron and turmeric. Set aside.

2. In the bottom of a flameproof tagine, heat oil over medium heat. Add onions and potatoes and cook, stirring, for 5 minutes. Add spice mixture and chicken, meaty side down, sliding around and moving vegetables away from bottom so that flesh is in direct contact with bottom of tagine. Cook for about 5 minutes or until chicken is browned on meaty side.

3. Using tongs, turn chicken over. Add broth and cinnamon stick and bring to a boil. Cover with tagine lid, reduce heat to low and simmer, stirring once, for 25 minutes.

4. Stir in chickpeas and parsley. Replace lid and simmer for 10 to 15 minutes or until chickpeas are heated through and chicken is longer pink inside for breasts and juices run clear for thighs. Discard cinnamon stick prior to serving.

Honey-Ginger Chicken with Walnuts and Prunes

Makes 4 servings

Make this richly flavored main dish and serve over couscous and all that is needed is a simple salad or blanched greens to complement the meal.

Tip

To toast nuts in a tagine: Measure walnuts into the bottom of a tagine. Toast over medium heat, stirring occasionally, for 3 to 4 minutes. Tip out into a separate bowl and let cool. No oil is needed.

● **Medium tagine**

3 tbsp	avocado or olive oil	45 mL
1	onion, coarsely chopped	1
1 tbsp	Berbere (page 42) or store-bought garam masala	15 mL
1 tbsp	chopped fresh or candied ginger	15 mL
4	skinless boneless chicken breasts (about 2 lbs/1 kg)	4
1/2 cup	chicken broth	125 mL
	Juice of 1 fresh lemon	
3 tbsp	liquid honey	45 mL
20	pitted prunes	20
20	toasted walnut halves (see Tip, left)	20

1. In the bottom of a flameproof tagine, heat oil over medium heat. Add onion, Berbere and ginger and cook, stirring, for 5 minutes. Add chicken, sliding breasts around and moving onions away from bottom so that flesh is in direct contact with bottom of tagine.

2. Add broth and lemon juice and bring to a boil. Stir in honey until incorporated. Cover with tagine lid, reduce heat to low and simmer for 25 minutes.

3. Stir in prunes and walnuts. Replace lid and simmer for 10 to 15 minutes or until prunes are plump and chicken is no longer pink inside.

Hot Spiced Quince Chicken

**Makes
4 servings**

Native to southwest Asia and now grown mostly in Turkey, the quince is a pome fruit similar to apples and pears. The bright, golden yellow, pear-shaped fruit is often used in Persian dishes, offering a sour or astringent taste to the overall complexity of the sauce. Tart apples are used in this dish when quinces are not available.

- ● **Medium tagine**
- ● **Baking sheet, lined with parchment or waxed paper**

4	skinless boneless chicken breasts, cut into thick strips (about 1½ lbs/750 g)	4
2 tbsp	Harissa (page 45) or hot pepper flakes	30 mL
3 tbsp	avocado or olive oil	45 mL
2	onions, cut in half and sliced	2
1	red bell pepper, cut into strips	1
1 tbsp	La Kama Spice Blend (page 44) or store-bought garam masala	15 mL
2	quince or tart apples, cut into eighths	2
1	can (28 oz/796 mL) diced tomatoes with juice	1
20	red or green seedless grapes, cut in half	20

1. Place chicken strips in one layer on prepared baking sheet. Distribute Harissa evenly over chicken and rub into the flesh. Cover tightly and set aside in refrigerator for 30 minutes or overnight. Let meat return to room temperature before cooking.

2. In the bottom of a flameproof tagine, heat oil over medium heat. Add onions, bell pepper and spice blend and cook, stirring, for 5 minutes. Add quince and cook, stirring, for 2 minutes. Add chicken strips, tomatoes with juice and grapes. Bring to a boil, cover with tagine lid, reduce heat to low and simmer, stirring once, for 20 to 25 minutes or until chicken is no longer pink inside.

Lemon Chicken with Mushrooms, Black Plums and Greens

Makes 4 servings

This is a mildly spiced chicken dish that is very delicately lemon-flavored and delicious over egg noodles or plain couscous. Even with their skins intact before cooking, the plums simply disappear into the sauce, adding to the complexity of the overall taste. You can remove the lemon pieces before serving the tagine if their slightly bitter taste is not to your liking.

Tip

If baby bok choy is not available, use one large bok choy, coarsely chopped.

● **Medium tagine**

3 tbsp	avocado or olive oil	45 mL
2 tbsp	butter	30 mL
1	onion, coarsely chopped	1
1 tbsp	Ras el Hanout (page 50) or store-bought	15 mL
4	skinless bone-in chicken breasts (about 3 lbs/1.5 kg)	4
4	cloves garlic, finely chopped	4
12	cremini mushrooms, cut in half	12
4	black or red plums, sliced	4
1 cup	chicken broth	250 mL
½	Preserved Lemon or Frozen Lemon (pages 48 and 49), chopped	½
2 tbsp	tahini	30 mL
4	baby bok choy or 2 cups (500 mL) shredded cabbage (see Tip, left)	4

1. In the bottom of a flameproof tagine, heat oil and melt butter over medium heat. Add onion and ras el hanout and cook, stirring, for 5 minutes. Add chicken, meaty side down, sliding breasts around and moving onions away from bottom so that flesh is in direct contact with bottom of tagine. Cook for about 5 minutes or until chicken is browned on meaty side.

2. Sprinkle garlic over chicken and onions. Using tongs, turn chicken over. Spread mushrooms and plums over chicken and onions and pour in broth. Add lemon rind and flesh and bring to a boil, stirring occasionally. Cover with tagine lid, reduce heat to low and simmer, stirring once, for 25 minutes.

3. Remove lid and stir in tahini until incorporated. Push bok choy into bubbling sauce to cover. Increase heat to medium-low to keep the sauce bubbling and simmer, uncovered, stirring occasionally and adjusting heat as necessary, for 10 to 12 minutes or until chicken is no longer pink inside and stems on bok choy are tender.

Pomegranate Chicken Tagine

Makes 4 to 6 servings

Make this in the fall when pomegranates are in season or substitute chopped plums in summer.

Tip

When buying pomegranates, select firm, bright red fruits that are free of bruising and feel heavy. Whole unpeeled pomegranates keep for up to 2 months in the crisper of the refrigerator. Whole seeds may be frozen and stored for up to 3 months. Pomegranate seeds are also available at Middle Eastern markets and specialty shops.

● **Medium or large tagine**

3 tbsp	avocado or olive oil	45 mL
2	onions, cut into quarters	2
4	cloves garlic	4
1 tbsp	Fennel Seasoning (page 43)	15 mL
1½ tsp	ground cinnamon	7 mL
1 tsp	hot pepper flakes, optional	5 mL
4	skinless boneless chicken breasts (about 2 lbs/1 kg)	4
	Juice of 1 fresh lemon	
3 cups	shredded cabbage	750 mL
2 tbsp	drained rinsed capers or diced olives	30 mL
2 tbsp	Pomegranate Molasses (page 172) or store-bought	30 mL
¾ cup	fresh pomegranate seeds (approx.) (see Tip, left)	175 mL

1. In the bottom of a flameproof tagine, heat oil over medium heat. Add onions, garlic, seasoning, cinnamon and hot pepper flakes and cook, stirring, for 5 minutes. Add chicken, sliding breasts around and moving onions away from bottom so that flesh is in direct contact with bottom of tagine. Cook for about 5 minutes or until chicken is browned on one side.

2. Using tongs, turn chicken and pour lemon juice over. Spread cabbage and capers over chicken. Drizzle with Pomegranate Molasses and bring liquids to a boil, stirring occasionally. Cover with tagine lid, reduce heat to low and simmer, stirring once, for 30 to 40 minutes or until cabbage is tender and chicken is no longer pink inside. Garnish with pomegranate seeds.

Rosemary Chicken and Potatoes

Makes 4 servings

Of all the North African herbs, rosemary is perhaps the most aromatic. Its piney scent permeates the air when this tagine is cooking.

Tip

Fresh or dried figs work in tagine dishes, but I tend to save the seasonal, fresh plump figs for eating out of hand and use the dried if they are to be chopped for tagine dishes. But for a true Mediterranean dish, fresh are best.

● **Medium tagine**

2 tbsp	avocado or olive oil	30 mL
2 tbsp	butter	30 mL
1	onion, cut into quarters	1
1 tbsp	Moroccan Cinnamon Spice Blend (page 47) or store-bought garam masala	15 mL
6	skinless bone-in chicken thighs (about 2 lbs/1 kg)	6
6	cloves garlic	6
3 tbsp	chopped fresh rosemary	45 mL
12	fingerling potatoes (about 1 lb/500 g)	12
2 cups	diced rutabaga	500 mL
2 tbsp	liquid honey	30 mL
¼ cup	chopped dried figs (see Tip, left)	60 mL

1. In the bottom of a flameproof tagine, heat oil and melt butter over medium heat. Add onion and spice blend and cook, stirring, for 5 minutes. Add chicken, meaty side down, sliding thighs around and moving onion away from bottom so that flesh is in direct contact with bottom of tagine. Cook for about 5 minutes or until chicken is browned on meaty side.

2. Using tongs, turn chicken over. Add garlic, rosemary and potatoes, tossing and stirring to coat chicken with oil and spices. Spread rutabaga over chicken and potatoes and drizzle honey over all. Cover with tagine lid, reduce heat to low and simmer, stirring once, for 25 minutes.

3. Stir in figs. Replace lid and simmer for 10 to 15 minutes or until figs are soft, rutabaga is tender and juices run clear when chicken is pierced with a fork.

Saffron Chicken with Squash and Cauliflower

Makes 4 to 6 servings

The saffron, red pepper and squash (you could also use pumpkin), give this dish a golden glow. Saffron not only colors the ingredients and the sauce but also gives a lightly floral essence to the taste.

Tip

If you do not have saffron, use 1 tbsp (15 mL) ground turmeric and add to the tagine when the spice blend is added.

● **Medium or large tagine**

	Juice of 1 fresh lemon	
25 to 30	saffron strands (see Tip, left)	25 to 30
3 tbsp	avocado or olive oil	45 mL
2	onions, cut into quarters	2
1	red bell pepper, chopped	2
1 tbsp	Ras el Hanout (page 50) or store-bought	15 mL
6	skinless bone-in chicken thighs (about 2 lbs/1 kg)	6
6	cloves garlic, coarsely chopped	6
2 cups	diced squash	500 mL
2 cups	sliced cauliflower florets	500 mL
	Flesh and rind of 1/2 Preserved Lemon (page 48), chopped, optional	

1. In a small bowl, pour lemon juice over saffron and set aside.

2. In the bottom of a flameproof tagine, heat oil over medium heat. Add onions, bell pepper and ras el hanout and cook, stirring, for 5 minutes. Add chicken, meaty side down, sliding thighs around and moving vegetables away from bottom so that flesh is in direct contact with bottom of tagine. Cook for about 5 minutes or until chicken is browned on the meaty side.

3. Sprinkle garlic over chicken and onions. Using tongs, turn chicken over. Spread squash and cauliflower over chicken and add Preserved Lemon flesh and rind, if using. Pour saffron mixture over and bring liquids to a boil, stirring occasionally. Cover with tagine lid, reduce heat to low and simmer, stirring once, for 30 to 40 minutes or until vegetables are tender, sauce is fragrant and juices run clear when chicken is pierced with a fork.

Sesame Chicken Tagine

**Makes
4 servings**

Carrots are added to
the tagine, making
this a one-dish meal. I
prefer to make my own
spice blends, but they
are available online
(see Sources, page 212)
or at Middle Eastern
food stores.

Tips

If you do not have Za'atar,
you can substitute the same
amount of dried oregano
or thyme.

Look for cracked green olives
at Middle Eastern or North
African stores because they
will be plump and make the
marinade authentic.

● **Medium tagine**

Marinade

	Juice of 1 fresh lemon	
2 tbsp	avocado or olive oil	30 mL
2 tbsp	toasted sesame oil	30 mL
3	cloves garlic, crushed	3
1	piece (1 inch/2.5 cm) fresh gingerroot, grated	1
4 to 6	skinless bone-in chicken thighs (about 2 lbs/1 kg)	4 to 6
2 tbsp	butter	30 mL
1 tbsp	avocado or olive oil	15 mL
1	onion, chopped	1
1 tbsp	Za'atar (page 54) or store-bought (see Tips, left)	15 mL
½ cup	chicken broth	125 mL
3	carrots, cut into 1-inch (2.5 cm) pieces	3
20	cracked green olives (see Tips, left)	20
1 tbsp	tahini	15 mL
3 tbsp	toasted sesame seeds	45 mL

1. *Marinade:* In a large bowl, combine lemon juice, avocado oil, sesame oil, garlic and ginger. Toss chicken thighs in the marinade, cover and refrigerate for 2 hours or overnight. Let meat return to room temperature before cooking.

2. In the bottom of a flameproof tagine, melt butter and heat oil over medium heat. Add onion and za'atar and cook, stirring, for 5 minutes. Add chicken broth, carrots, green olives, chicken and marinade. Bring liquids to a boil, cover with tagine lid, reduce heat to low and simmer, stirring once, for 30 to 40 minutes or until juices run clear when chicken is pierced with a fork.

3. Stir in tahini until incorporated. Garnish with sesame seeds.

Spiced Chicken and Lentil Tagine

Makes 4 servings

Once only available in Middle Eastern and North African food stores, sumac is now found in fine cookware and food stores in North America. Whole or ground sumac berries are fruity-tart, contributing the astringent spike in this tagine.

Tips

I like the French blue-green, Puy lentils and the tiny golden lentils, but any variety will work.

If sumac is not available, use whole or ground pomegranate seeds instead.

Caution: Purchase sumac from specialist grocery stores selling Middle Eastern ingredients. Some members of the sumac family (found mostly in North America) have poisonous berries.

● **Medium tagine**

1 cup	green, brown or yellow lentils (see Tips, left)	250 mL
3 cups	water	750 mL
3	skinless boneless chicken breasts (about 1½ lbs/750 g)	3
3 tbsp	avocado or olive oil	45 mL
1	onion, cut into quarters	1
1 tbsp	Ras el Hanout (page 50) or store-bought	15 mL
3	cloves garlic, crushed	3
12	cherry tomatoes, cut in half	12
2 tsp	ground sumac or pomegranate seeds (see Tips, left)	10 mL
1 tsp	hot pepper flakes, optional	5 mL
2 cups	diced squash or pumpkin	500 mL
½ cup	chopped dates	125 mL

1. Using a sieve, rinse and drain lentils. In a saucepan, combine lentils and water and bring to a boil over high heat. Skim off any foam. Cover, reduce heat to low and simmer for 15 to 20 minutes or until tender. Drain, rinse and set aside.

2. Meanwhile, cut chicken into 1-inch (2.5 cm) pieces and set aside. In the bottom of a flameproof tagine, heat oil over medium heat. Add onion and ras el hanout and cook, stirring, for 5 minutes. Add garlic, tomatoes, sumac, and hot pepper flakes, if using and cook, stirring, for 2 minutes. Add chicken and squash and toss to coat in vegetables and spices. Cover with tagine lid, reduce heat to low and simmer, stirring once, for 25 minutes.

3. Stir in lentils and dates. Replace lid and simmer for 10 to 15 minutes or until dates are melted into the sauce, squash is tender and chicken is no longer pink inside.

Spiced Duck Tagine with Pears and Plums

Makes 4 to 6 servings

Duck makes this a special-occasion tagine, but you can use chicken, Cornish game hens, pheasant or quails.

Tip

For the duck meat, you can use breasts, thighs or legs.

- Medium or large tagine
- Baking sheet, lined with parchment or waxed paper

2 lbs	skinless boneless duck meat (see Tip, left)	1 kg
1 tbsp	Tabil Spice Blend (page 53) or ground coriander	15 mL
3 tbsp	avocado or olive oil	45 mL
2	onions, cut into quarters	2
1 tbsp	Tunisian Five Spices (page 54) or store-bought garam masala	15 mL
2	pears, cut into 8 wedges	2
2	plums or nectarines, cut into quarters	2
¼ cup	chicken broth	60 mL
2 tbsp	liquid honey	30 mL
¼ cup	raisins	60 mL

1. In a large bowl, toss duck meat with Tabil Spice Blend to coat. Set aside.

2. In the bottom of a flameproof tagine, heat oil over medium heat. Add onions and Tunisian spice blend and cook, stirring, for 5 minutes. Add spiced duck, pears and plums and cook, stirring, for about 5 minutes or until duck is lightly browned.

3. Add chicken broth and bring to a boil, stirring occasionally. Stir in honey until incorporated. Cover with tagine lid, reduce heat to low and simmer, stirring once, for 25 minutes.

4. Stir in raisins. Replace lid and simmer for 10 to 15 minutes or until raisins are plump, vegetables are tender and duck is no longer pink inside for breasts and juices run clear for thighs.

Turkey Breasts with Pomegranate-Walnut Sauce

Makes 4 servings

Walnut paste, made with pomegranate juice, is used for both flavor and to thicken the sauce in this tagine.

Tip

I recommend the use of organic, cold-pressed extra virgin avocado oil in the tagine recipes in this book because it is excellent for medium to high heat cooking. Unlike other polyunsaturated oils, olive oil in particular, avocado oil does not break down under high heat cooking. It is an excellent source of vitamin E and contains beneficial omega-3, 6 and 9 fatty acids.

Variation

Use duck meat or chicken in place of the turkey.

- Medium tagine
- Food processor

1 cup	chopped walnuts	250 mL
1 cup	pomegranate juice	250 mL
2 tbsp	avocado or olive oil (see Tip, left)	30 mL
1	onion, chopped	1
1 tbsp	Moroccan Cinnamon Spice Blend (page 47) or store-bought garam masala	15 mL
1	skinless boneless turkey breast (about 2 lbs/1 kg)	1
3	cloves garlic, chopped	3
2 tbsp	Pomegranate Molasses (page 172) or store-bought	30 mL
¼ cup	ground pomegranate seeds, optional	60 mL

1. In the bottom of a flameproof tagine, toast walnuts over medium heat for 1 to 2 minutes or until slightly colored. Let cool. In a food processor, chop walnuts and, with motor running, add pomegranate juice through opening in lid. Blend until smooth. Set aside.

2. In the bottom of the same flameproof tagine, heat oil over medium heat. Add onion and spice blend and cook, stirring, for 5 minutes. Add turkey, sliding breast around and moving onions away from bottom so that flesh is in direct contact with bottom of tagine. Cook, turning frequently, for 8 to 10 minutes or until turkey is browned on both sides.

3. Add garlic and walnut paste and bring to a simmer, stirring occasionally. Stir in pomegranate molasses until incorporated. Cover with tagine lid, reduce heat to low and simmer, stirring once, for 35 to 45 minutes or until turkey is no longer pink inside. Carve turkey and replace slices in tagine with sauce or carve at the table and serve sauce separately. Garnish with pomegranate seeds, if using.

Lamb

Chermoula Baked Lamb with Peppers and Pomegranates

**Makes
6 servings**

Here is where Chermoula spice paste really shines as a rub for long-cooking meats. In this recipe, the spice paste serves to flavor both the meat and the cooking sauce.

Tip

Whole pomegranate seeds may be frozen and stored for up to 3 months. Pomegranate seeds are also available at Middle Eastern markets and specialty shops.

- **Large tagine**
- **Preheat oven to 350°F (180°C)**

1½ lbs	bone-in lamb leg	750 g
3	cloves garlic, cut into slivers	3
¾ cup	Chermoula Moroccan Rub (page 40)	175 mL
3 tbsp	avocado or olive oil	45 mL
1	onion, cut into quarters	1
2	red bell peppers, cut into large pieces	2
2 tsp	Moroccan Cinnamon Spice Blend (page 47) or store-bought garam masala	10 mL
¾ cup	beef or chicken broth	175 mL
2 cups	cooked red lentils (see Tips, right)	500 mL
1 cup	pomegranate seeds (see Tip, left)	250 mL
¼ cup	Pomegranate Molasses (page 172) or store bought	60 mL
¼ cup	sesame seeds	60 mL

1. With a sharp knife, make slits in the flesh of the lamb and insert garlic slivers. Place lamb on a baking sheet and rub Chermoula paste over. Cover tightly and set aside in the refrigerator for at least 6 hours or overnight. Let meat return to room temperature before cooking.

2. In the bottom of a flameproof tagine, heat oil over medium heat. Add onion and cook, stirring, for 5 minutes. Add bell peppers and spice blend and cook, stirring constantly, for 2 minutes. Add lamb, sliding around and moving vegetables away from bottom so that flesh is in direct contact with bottom of tagine. Cook for about 5 minutes or until lamb is browned on one side.

Tips

Some tagines have a tendency to spatter liquids if the lid is loose fitting. To avoid a messy oven bottom, place a baking sheet under the tagine when using in the oven and check liquids at least once and add more broth if needed.

To cook lentils: In a strainer, pick over and remove any small stones or grit from 1 cup (250 mL) red or brown dried lentils. In a saucepan, cover lentils with water allowing a good 1 inch (2.5 cm) over top of them. Bring to a boil over high heat. Cover and reduce heat to medium-low and simmer for 15 minutes or until tender. Drain and rinse under cool water. Makes 2 cups (500 mL).

3. Using a meat fork, turn lamb so that browned side is up. Add broth and bring to a boil. Cover with tagine lid, and bake in preheated oven, turning lamb once, for $1\frac{1}{2}$ hours. Stir in lentils and pomegranate seeds and drizzle pomegranate molasses over lamb. Return to oven and bake, uncovered, for 30 to 45 minutes or until lamb is tender and falling away from the bone. Garnish with sesame seeds.

Cinnamon Lamb Tagine with Apricots

Makes 4 to 6 servings

Cinnamon is one of the key ingredients in North African spice blends. Here its sweetness is balanced by the tartness of the dried apricots.

Tip

For this quantity of cooked chickpeas, soak and cook 1/2 cup (125 mL) dried chickpeas or use 1 cup (250 mL) canned, drained and rinsed.

● **Medium or large tagine**

3 tbsp	avocado or olive oil	45 mL
1	onion, cut into quarters	1
1 tbsp	Moroccan Cinnamon Spice Blend (page 47) or store-bought garam masala	15 mL
1½ lbs	boneless lamb leg, trimmed and cubed	750 g
2	cloves garlic, chopped	2
1	can (14 oz/398 mL) diced tomatoes with juice	1
2	carrots, cut into coins	2
1	medium zucchini, chopped	1
½ cup	sliced dried apricots	125 mL
1 cup	cooked chickpeas, drained (see Tip, left)	250 mL
1 tbsp	liquid honey	15 mL

1. In the bottom of a flameproof tagine, heat oil over medium heat. Add onion and cook, stirring, for 5 minutes. Add spice blend, lamb and garlic, stirring to coat lamb with vegetables and seasonings. Cook, stirring occasionally, for 6 to 7 minutes or until lamb is browned on all sides.

2. Add tomatoes with juice, carrots, zucchini and apricots and bring liquids to a boil, stirring frequently. Cover with tagine lid, reduce heat to low and simmer, stirring occasionally, for 1 hour.

3. Stir in chickpeas and honey, replace lid and simmer for 15 to 20 minutes or until lamb is tender. Lamb should cut easily with a fork and if not quite tender, replace cover and simmer until tender.

Fruited Lamb Tagine

Makes 4 to 6 servings

Ground almonds are used in this tagine as a thickener, but they do impart a very delicate flavor as well.

Tip

Use pears in the fall when they are plentiful. At other times peaches, apricots, apples, quinces, plums or 1 cup (250 mL) mixed dried fruit can be substituted, and in a pinch, drained canned fruit may be added in the last 15 minutes.

● **Small or medium tagine**

2 tbsp	avocado or olive oil	30 mL
2	onions, coarsely chopped	2
2 tsp	grated fresh gingerroot	10 mL
1 tsp	ground coriander	5 mL
1 tsp	ground cinnamon	5 mL
1 tsp	ground cumin	5 mL
2 lbs	boneless lamb (shoulder or leg), trimmed and cubed	1 kg
4	pears, cut into quarters (see Tip, left)	4
¼ cup	coarsely ground almonds	60 mL
1 tbsp	liquid honey	15 mL

1. In the bottom of a flameproof tagine, heat oil over medium heat. Add onions and cook, stirring, for 5 minutes. Add ginger, coriander, cinnamon and cumin and cook, stirring constantly, for 1 minute. Add lamb and stir to coat with seasonings. Cook, stirring occasionally, for 6 to 7 minutes or until lamb is browned on all sides.

2. Add enough water to cover the lamb and bring to a boil, stirring frequently. Cover with tagine lid, reduce heat to low and simmer, stirring occasionally, for 1 hour.

3. Stir in pears, almonds and honey. Replace lid and simmer for 15 to 20 minutes or until both fruit and lamb are tender. Lamb should cut easily with a fork and if not quite tender, replace cover and simmer until tender.

Gingered Lamb Tagine with Figs

Makes 4 to 6 servings

The pears and figs morph into a rich and delicately sweet sauce that is balanced by the Berbere seasoning.

Tip

I recommend the use of organic, cold-pressed extra virgin avocado oil in the tagine recipes in this book because it is excellent for medium to high heat cooking. Unlike other polyunsaturated oils, olive oil in particular, avocado oil does not break down under high heat cooking. It is an excellent source of vitamin E and contains beneficial omega-3, 6 and 9 fatty acids.

● **Small or medium tagine**

2 tbsp	avocado or olive oil	30 mL
2	onions, coarsely chopped	2
1 tbsp	Berbere (page 42)	15 mL
1 tbsp	finely chopped candied ginger	15 mL
2 tsp	grated fresh gingerroot	10 mL
2 lbs	boneless lamb (shoulder or leg), trimmed and cubed	1 kg
2 cups	cauliflower florets	500 mL
2	pears, cut into quarters (see Tip, page 81)	2
8 oz	dried or fresh figs, cut in half	250 g
1 tbsp	liquid honey	15 mL

1. In the bottom of a flameproof tagine, heat oil over medium heat. Add onions and cook, stirring, for 5 minutes. Add Berbere, candied ginger and fresh ginger and cook, stirring constantly, for 1 minute. Add lamb and stir to coat with seasonings. Cook, stirring occasionally, for 6 to 7 minutes or until lamb is browned on all sides.

2. Add cauliflower, pears, figs and enough water to cover the lamb. Bring to a boil, stirring frequently. Cover with tagine lid, reduce heat to low and simmer, stirring occasionally, for 1 hour.

3. Stir in honey. Replace lid and simmer for 15 to 20 minutes or until lamb is tender. Lamb should cut easily with a fork and if not quite tender, replace cover and simmer until tender.

Lamb and Chestnut Tagine

Makes 4 to 6 servings

Meaty chestnuts are considered to be a starch component in tagine dishes. Look for roasted, peeled fresh or frozen chestnuts in specialty stores.

Variation

You may substitute natural almonds for the chestnuts.

● **Small or medium tagine**

2 tbsp	avocado or olive oil	30 mL
6	small shallots	6
4	cloves garlic, chopped	4
1 cup	mushroom halves	250 mL
1 tbsp	La Kama Spice Blend (page 44) or store-bought garam masala	15 mL
2 lbs	boneless lamb (shoulder or leg), trimmed and cubed	1 kg
¾ cup	beef or chicken broth	175 mL
1 cup	quartered Brussels sprouts	250 mL
8 oz	peeled chestnuts	250 g
1 tbsp	Pomegranate Molasses (page 172) or store bought	15 mL

1. In the bottom of a flameproof tagine, heat oil over medium heat. Add shallots and cook, stirring, for 5 minutes. Add garlic, mushrooms and spice blend and cook, stirring constantly, for 2 minutes.

2. Add lamb and stir to coat with vegetables and spice blend. Add broth and bring to a boil. Stir in Brussels sprouts. Cover with tagine lid, reduce heat to low and simmer, stirring occasionally, for 1 hour.

3. Stir in chestnuts and pomegranate molasses. Replace lid and simmer for 15 to 20 minutes or until lamb is tender. Lamb should cut easily with a fork and if not quite tender, replace cover and simmer until tender.

Lamb and Mushrooms with Leeks and Dates

Makes 4 to 6 servings

Mushrooms add an earthy note to this tagine, which also draws on three alliums for its depth of flavor.

● **Medium or large tagine**

2 tbsp	avocado or olive oil	30 mL
6	small shallots	6
1 tbsp	butter	15 mL
2 cups	sliced mushrooms	500 mL
2	leeks, white and light green parts, sliced	2
4	cloves garlic, chopped	4
1 tbsp	Ras el Hanout (page 50) or store-bought	15 mL
2 lbs	boneless lamb (shoulder or leg), trimmed and cubed	1 kg
1 cup	beef or chicken broth	250 mL
1 cup	chopped dates	250 mL
¼ cup	coarsely ground almonds	60 mL
1 tbsp	liquid honey	15 mL

1. In the bottom of a flameproof tagine, heat oil over medium heat. Add shallots and cook, stirring, for 5 minutes. Add butter, mushrooms, leeks, garlic and ras el hanout and cook, stirring constantly, for 2 minutes. Cover with tagine lid, reduce heat to low and simmer for 6 to 7 minutes or until mushrooms are tender crisp and still holding their shape.

2. Add lamb and stir to coat with seasonings. Add broth and dates and bring to a boil, stirring frequently. Cover with tagine lid, reduce heat to low and simmer, stirring occasionally, for 1 hour.

3. Stir in almonds and honey. Replace lid and simmer for 15 to 20 minutes or until lamb is tender. Lamb should cut easily with a fork and if not quite tender, replace cover and simmer until tender.

Lamb and Peaches with Toasted Nuts and Seeds

Makes 4 servings

Not the usual spices here, rather fresh rosemary, the herb that best complements lamb, is used with dried oregano (in the Za'atar) for a green and slightly piney flavor.

Tip

This recipe calls for center slices or arm chops, which look very similar. They are usually thinly cut slices from either the center of the lamb leg or the arm and are round (or oblong) with a round bone in the center or at one end. You can also use lamb loin or double loin chops in this recipe.

● **Small or medium tagine**

1 tbsp	butter	15 mL
1/2 cup	almond slivers	125 mL
1/4 cup	sesame seeds	60 mL
2 tbsp	avocado or olive oil	30 mL
1	onion, quartered	1
2	cloves garlic, chopped	2
1 tbsp	chopped fresh rosemary	15 mL
1 tbsp	Za'atar (page 54) or store-bought	15 mL
2 lbs	bone-in lamb center slices or lamb arm chops (see Tip, left)	1 kg
1	can (14 oz/398 mL) sliced peaches with juice	1

1. In the bottom of a flameproof tagine, melt butter over medium heat. Add almonds and toast, stirring constantly, for 1 minute or until they begin to color slightly. Stir in sesame seeds and toast, stirring constantly, for 30 seconds or until light golden. Tip into a bowl and set aside.

2. Add oil to bottom of tagine and heat over medium heat. Add onion and cook, stirring, for 5 minutes. Add garlic, rosemary and za'atar and cook, stirring constantly, for 30 seconds. Add lamb, sliding around and moving onions away from bottom so that flesh is in direct contact with bottom of tagine. Cook for about 3 minutes or until browned on one side.

3. Using tongs, turn chops over. Add peaches with juice. Cover with tagine lid, reduce heat to low and simmer for 30 to 45 minutes or until lamb is tender. Lamb should cut easily with a fork and if not quite tender, replace cover and simmer until tender. Sprinkle toasted almonds and sesame seeds over top.

Lamb Shanks in Persian Tomato Sauce

Makes 4 servings

With its sweet-sour flavor, the sauce is simmered with the shanks until both are rich with the tastes of ancient Persia.

- **Medium or large tagine**

¼ cup	all-purpose flour	60 mL
1 tbsp	Bahrat Spice Blend (page 39) or store-bought garam masala	15 mL
4	lamb shanks (see Tips, right)	4
1 tbsp	butter	15 mL
½ cup	almond slivers	125 mL
¼ cup	sesame seeds	60 mL
2 tbsp	avocado or olive oil	30 mL
1	onion, quartered	1
3	cloves garlic, slivered	3
3 tbsp	chopped fresh parsley	45 mL
1 tbsp	chopped fresh rosemary	15 mL
1	can (28 oz/796 mL) whole plum (Roma) tomatoes with juice	1
1 cup	pitted prunes	250 mL
½ cup	chopped dates	125 mL
¼ cup	liquid honey	60 mL

1. In a bowl, combine flour and spice blend. Dredge shanks in flour mixture, turning to coat all sides. Set aside.

2. In the bottom of a flameproof tagine, melt butter over medium heat. Add almonds and toast, stirring constantly, for 1 minute or until they begin to color slightly. Stir in sesame seeds and cook, stirring constantly, for 30 seconds or until light golden. Tip into a bowl and set aside.

3. Add oil to bottom of tagine and heat over medium heat. Add onion and cook, stirring, for 5 minutes. Add garlic, parsley and rosemary and cook, stirring constantly, for 30 seconds. Add floured shanks, sliding around and moving onions away from bottom so that flesh is in direct contact with bottom of tagine. Cook for about 3 minutes or until browned on one side.

Tips

Lamb shanks are considered a "tougher" cut of meat and so are perfect for the long, slow and moist cooking in a tagine. Cut from the arm of the shoulder of the animal, shanks usually contain the ball and socket bones of the leg and shoulder, with the surrounding flesh covered in a thin layer of fat.

Lamb shanks may vary in size. If your tagine is medium in size, look for smaller shanks that will fit in the bottom in one layer.

4. Using tongs, turn shanks over. Add tomatoes with juice, prunes and dates. Cover with tagine lid, reduce heat to low and simmer, turning lamb once, for $1\frac{1}{2}$ hours or until lamb is tender. Lamb should separate easily from the bone and if not quite tender, replace cover and simmer for 20 to 30 minutes or until tender. Drizzle honey over shanks and sprinkle toasted almonds and sesame seeds over all.

Lamb Tagine with Grapes and Caramelized Onions

**Makes
4 servings**

Purple grapes and red wine combine with caramelized onions to give this tagine the taste of a long-simmered stew. You can cook in a flameproof tagine on top of the stove in less time, but the long, slow oven simmering is what brings out the best flavors.

● **Large or medium tagine**

2 tbsp	avocado or olive oil	30 mL
2	onions, halved and sliced	2
6	cloves garlic	6
2 tsp	ground cumin	10 mL
1 tsp	ground ginger	5 mL
4	lamb medallions (about 1 lb/500 g)	4
¾ cup	beef or chicken broth	175 mL
½ cup	red wine	125 mL
1	carrot, coarsely chopped	1
1	zucchini, coarsely chopped	1
24	purple seedless grapes, quartered	24
12	marinated olives, drained and quartered	12

1. In the bottom of a flameproof tagine, heat oil over medium heat. Add onions and garlic, and cook, stirring frequently, for 10 to 15 minutes or until soft and golden. Stir in cumin and ginger. Add lamb, sliding medallions around and moving onions away from the bottom so that the flesh is in direct contact with the bottom of the tagine. Cook for 1 to 2 minutes or until lamb is browned on one side. Turn and brown on the other side.

2. Add beef broth and wine and bring to a boil. Stir in carrot and zucchini. Cover with tagine lid, reduce heat to low and simmer, turning medallions once, for 1 hour. Stir in grapes and olives. Replace lid and simmer for 10 minutes or until heated through. Lamb should cut easily with a fork and if not quite tender, replace cover and simmer until tender.

Lamb Tagine with Mediterranean Vegetables

Makes 6 to 8 servings

Squash and pumpkin are widely used in both vegetable and meat tagine dishes.

● **Large tagine**

3 tbsp	avocado or olive oil	45 mL
2	onions, quartered	2
4	cloves garlic, coarsely chopped	4
1 tbsp	Bahrat Spice Blend (page 39) or store-bought garam masala	15 mL
2 lbs	boneless lamb (shoulder or leg), trimmed and cut into cubes	1 kg
¾ cup	beef or chicken broth	175 mL
3 tbsp	freshly squeezed lemon juice	45 mL
2	carrots, coarsely chopped	2
2	zucchini, diced	2
1 cup	diced rutabaga or turnip	250 mL
1 cup	diced squash or pumpkin	250 mL
⅓ cup	raisins	75 mL
1	can (14 to 19 oz/398 to 540 mL) chickpeas, drained and rinsed	1
1	can (14 oz/398 mL) artichokes, drained	1

1. In the bottom of a flameproof tagine, heat oil over medium heat. Add onions and cook, stirring, for 5 minutes. Add garlic and spice blend and cook, stirring frequently, for 2 minutes. Stir in lamb, tossing to coat with onions and spices. Cook, stirring constantly, for 6 to 7 minutes or until lamb is browned on all sides.

2. Add beef broth and lemon juice and bring to a boil. Stir in carrots, zucchini, rutabaga, squash and raisins. Cover with tagine lid, reduce heat to low and simmer, stirring occasionally, for 1 hour. Stir in chickpeas and artichokes. Replace lid and simmer for 10 to 15 minutes or until lamb is tender and artichokes are heated through. Lamb should cut easily with a fork and if not quite tender, replace cover and simmer until tender.

Lamb Tagine with Oranges and Dates

Makes 4 to 6 servings

The tart, fresh citrus taste of oranges in this tagine dish is subtle yet refreshing.

Tip

Citrus fruit works to balance the richness of lamb, so use lemons and oranges and grapefruit often. You can simply add them in the last 15 minutes of cooking the tagine.

Variation

You can use 1 cup (250 mL) coarsely chopped figs for the dates.

- **Medium tagine**
- **Preheat oven to 350°F (180°C)**

2 tbsp	avocado or olive oil	30 mL
2	onions, quartered	2
1 tbsp	Berbere (page 42) or store-bought garam masala	15 mL
2 lbs	boneless lamb (shoulder or leg), trimmed and cut into cubes	1 kg
¾ cup	beef or chicken broth	175 mL
3 tbsp	freshly squeezed lemon juice	45 mL
2	carrots, coarsely chopped	2
2 cups	shredded green cabbage	500 mL
1 cup	pitted medjool dates	250 mL
2	oranges, sectioned	2

1. In the bottom of a flameproof tagine, heat oil over medium heat. Add onions and Berbere and cook, stirring, for 5 minutes. Add lamb, tossing to coat with onions and spices. Cook, stirring constantly, for 6 to 7 minutes or until lamb is browned on all sides.

2. Add beef broth and lemon juice and bring to a boil. Stir in carrots, cabbage and dates. Cover with tagine lid, reduce heat to low and simmer, stirring occasionally, for 1 hour. Stir in orange sections. Replace lid and simmer for 10 minutes or until heated through. Lamb should cut easily with a fork and if not quite tender, replace cover and simmer until tender.

Lamb with Apricots, Tamarind and Pistachios

Makes 4 to 6 servings

Tamarind is found in Middle Eastern food shops. It adds a sour note to the sweet fruit in this tagine.

Tip

Tamarind is sold in Indian and Middle Eastern food stores in two forms: semi-dried, a sticky mass of broken pods with fibers and beans; or as a moist vacuum-packed fibrous pulp. Be sure to check the tamarind for seeds. They are very smooth and hard and easy to miss but a hazard for teeth in a finished dish.

● **Medium or large tagine**

2 tbsp	avocado or olive oil	30 mL
2	onions, quartered	2
1 tbsp	Berbere (page 42) or store-bought garam masala	15 mL
2 lbs	boneless lamb (shoulder or leg), trimmed and cut into cubes	1 kg
1 tbsp	chopped pitted tamarind (see Tip, left)	15 mL
¾ cup	beef or chicken broth	175 mL
3 tbsp	freshly squeezed lemon juice	45 mL
2	zucchini, coarsely chopped	2
1 cup	slivered dried apricots	250 mL
½ cup	pistachio nuts	125 mL

1. In the bottom of a flameproof tagine, heat oil over medium heat. Add onions and Berbere and cook, stirring, for 5 minutes. Add lamb and tamarind, tossing to coat with onions and spices. Cook, stirring constantly, for 6 to 7 minutes or until lamb is browned on all sides.

2. Add beef broth and lemon juice and bring to a boil. Stir in zucchini and apricots. Cover with tagine lid, reduce heat to low and simmer, stirring occasionally, for 1 hour. Stir in pistachio nuts. Replace lid and simmer for 10 minutes or until heated through. Lamb should cut easily with a fork and if not quite tender, replace cover and simmer until tender.

Lamb with Potatoes, Olives and Rosemary

Makes 4 to 6 servings

Rosemary (*Rosemarius officinalis*) grows wild all over the Mediterranean and is a key flavor for lamb.

Tip

Whenever you must substitute dried green herbs for fresh, use half the amount of fresh called for in the recipe.

● **Medium or large tagine**

3 tbsp	avocado or olive oil	45 mL
1	onion, quartered	1
3	cloves garlic, coarsely chopped	3
2 tbsp	chopped fresh rosemary	30 mL
2 lbs	boneless lamb (shoulder or leg), trimmed and cubed	1 kg
2	large potatoes, cut into wedges	2
1 cup	beef or chicken broth	250 mL
1 cup	pitted green olives	250 mL

1. In the bottom of a flameproof tagine, heat oil over medium heat. Add onion, garlic and rosemary and cook, stirring, for 5 minutes. Add lamb, tossing to coat with onions and herbs. Cook, stirring constantly, for 10 to 12 minutes or until lamb is browned on all sides.

2. Add potatoes and beef broth and bring to a boil. Cover with tagine lid, reduce heat to low and simmer for 1 hour. Stir in olives. Replace lid and simmer for 10 minutes or until heated through. Lamb should cut easily with a fork and if not quite tender, replace cover and simmer until tender.

Minted Lamb Tagine

Makes 4 to 6 servings

Fresh spearmint (*Mentha crispa*) is an important herb in North Africa for both tea and flavoring tagine dishes as well as desserts.

Tip

I recommend the use of organic, cold-pressed extra virgin avocado oil in the tagine recipes in this book because it is excellent for medium to high heat cooking. Unlike other polyunsaturated oils, olive oil in particular, avocado oil does not break down under high heat cooking. It is an excellent source of vitamin E and contains beneficial omega-3, 6 and 9 fatty acids.

● **Medium or large tagine**

3 tbsp	avocado or olive oil	45 mL
1	onion, quartered	1
3	cloves garlic, coarsely chopped	3
1 tbsp	Ras el Hanout (page 50) or store-bought	15 mL
2 lbs	boneless lamb (shoulder or leg), trimmed and cubed	1 kg
¾ cup	beef or chicken broth	175 mL
6	okra, sliced	6
2	zucchini, diced	2
1	red bell pepper, diced	1
½ cup	chopped fresh mint	125 mL

1. In the bottom of a flameproof tagine, heat oil over medium heat. Add onion, garlic and ras el hanout and cook, stirring, for 5 minutes. Add lamb, tossing to coat with onion and seasoning. Cook, stirring occasionally, for 6 to 7 minutes or until lamb is browned on all sides.

2. Add broth and bring to a boil. Cover with tagine lid, reduce heat to low and simmer, stirring once or twice, for 1 hour. Stir in okra, zucchini, bell pepper and mint. Replace lid and simmer for 15 to 20 minutes or until vegetables and lamb are tender. Lamb should cut easily with a fork and if not quite tender, replace cover and simmer until tender.

Meatballs in Herbed Lemon Sauce

Makes 4 servings

Kefta, or meatballs, are not usually browned; instead they are gently coaxed to cooked perfection in a gently simmering sauce. This sauce, with its bright lemon taste, is thick and rich with green herbs of the Mediterranean.

- Medium tagine
- Rimmed baking sheet, lined with parchment paper

Meatballs

1 lb	lean ground lamb	500 g
1/2 cup	finely chopped onion	125 mL
1/2 cup	fresh bread crumbs	125 mL
3 tbsp	chopped fresh parsley	45 mL
1 tsp	sea salt	5 mL
1/2 tsp	ground cumin	2 mL
1/2 tsp	paprika	2 mL
1/4 tsp	ground nutmeg	1 mL
1	egg	1

Sauce

2 tbsp	avocado or olive oil	30 mL
1	onion, coarsely chopped	1
1 tbsp	Ras el Hanout (page 50) or store-bought	15 mL
3/4 cup	beef or chicken broth	175 mL
1 cup	shredded carrots	250 mL
1/4 cup	chopped sun-dried tomatoes	60 mL
1/2	Preserved Lemon or Frozen Lemon (pages 48 and 49), chopped, or 3 tbsp (45 mL) freshly squeezed lemon juice	1/2
2 tbsp	chopped fresh parsley	30 mL
2 tbsp	chopped fresh cilantro	30 mL
2 tsp	chopped fresh rosemary	10 mL

1. *Meatballs:* In a bowl, using lightly oiled hands, combine ground lamb, onion, bread crumbs, parsley, salt, cumin, paprika and nutmeg. Add egg and knead until a paste-like consistency.

2. Scoop out 1 tbsp (15 mL) of lamb mixture and roll into walnut-size balls. Use immediately or place on prepared baking sheet, tightly cover with plastic wrap and refrigerate for up to 1 day in advance. Bring to room temperature to cook.

Variation

Use ground turkey, chicken or beef in place of the ground lamb in this recipe.

3. *Sauce:* In the bottom of a flameproof tagine, heat oil over medium heat. Add onion and ras el hanout and cook, stirring, for 5 minutes. Add broth and bring to a boil. Stir in carrots, sun-dried tomatoes, Preserved Lemon, parsley, cilantro and rosemary.

4. Gently lower meatballs into simmering sauce. Cover with tagine lid, reduce heat to low and gently simmer, stirring once, for 45 minutes, until meatballs are cooked right through, showing no signs of pink. If not cooked, replace cover and simmer for 10 to 20 minutes or until cooked.

Saffron Lamb Tagine with Squash and Olives

Makes 4 to 6 servings

Everything glows with a golden hue in this one-pot meal. Use pumpkin or a firm squash variety such as acorn or butternut.

● **Medium or large tagine**

20	strands saffron	20
3 tbsp	avocado or olive oil, divided	45 mL
2	onions, coarsely chopped	2
1 tbsp	Bahrat Spice Blend (page 39)	15 mL
4	cloves garlic, sliced	4
2 lbs	boneless lamb (shoulder or leg), trimmed and cubed	1 kg
2 cups	squash cubes	500 mL
½ cup	chopped green olives	125 mL

1. In a small bowl, combine saffron with 1 tbsp (15 mL) of oil. Set aside.

2. In the bottom of a flameproof tagine, heat remaining oil over medium heat. Add onions and cook, stirring, for 5 minutes. Add spice blend and garlic and cook, stirring constantly, for 1 minute. Add lamb and saffron mixture and stir to coat with seasonings. Cook, stirring occasionally, for 6 to 7 minutes or until lamb is browned on all sides.

3. Add enough water to cover the lamb and bring to a boil, stirring frequently. Stir in squash. Cover with tagine lid, reduce heat to low and simmer, stirring occasionally, for 1 hour.

4. Stir in olives. Replace lid and simmer for 10 minutes or until heated through. Lamb should cut easily with a fork and if not quite tender, replace cover and simmer until tender.

Beef

Beef and Root Vegetable Tagine

Makes about 6 servings

Spiced beef simmered in red wine and broth makes this hearty tagine worthy of the coldest months of the year. Using beef cut in strips similar to those used in stir-fried dishes exposes more of the meat to the moist heat and renders it tender in less time than thicker cuts.

Tips

Use 2 cups (500 mL) cooked chickpeas or 1 can as directed in the recipe.

Most meat departments of major supermarkets sell pre-cut stewing beef, but it may not be trimmed to your preference. If you prefer to trim and cut your own beef for stewing, you can purchase chuck, round or flank cuts.

● **Large tagine**

2 tbsp	avocado or olive oil	30 mL
2	onions, cut into quarters	2
1 tbsp	Berbere (page 42) or store-bought garam masala	15 mL
1 tsp	Ras el Hanout (page 50) or store-bought	5 mL
2 lbs	stewing beef, cut into $\frac{1}{2}$-inch (1 cm) strips (see Tips, left)	1 kg
2	carrots, cut into 1-inch (2.5 cm) pieces	2
2	parsnips, cut into 1-inch (2.5 cm) pieces	2
$\frac{3}{4}$ cup	beef broth	175 mL
$\frac{1}{4}$ cup	red wine	60 mL
1	can (14 to 19 oz/398 to 540 mL) chickpeas, drained and rinsed (see Tips, left)	1
1 cup	chopped dates	250 mL

1. In the bottom of a flameproof tagine, heat oil over medium heat. Add onions, Berbere and ras el hanout and cook, stirring, for 5 minutes. Add beef and cook, stirring frequently, for about 5 minutes. Meat will not brown, but the spices will infuse it during this cooking time.

2. Add carrots, parsnips, broth and wine and bring to a boil. Cover with tagine lid, reduce heat to low and simmer, stirring occasionally, for 1 hour. Stir in chickpeas and dates, replace lid and simmer for 10 to 15 minutes. Beef should cut easily with a fork and if not quite tender, replace cover and simmer until beef is tender.

Beef, Leek and Onion Tagine

 Makes about 6 servings

Dredging meat in flour is a technique that is more European and North American than Moroccan. In this recipe, I use it to thicken the tagine and the meat is not browned as it would be in Western-style stew. The spices in this dish are subtle and there is a lot of meat; in fact the meat may easily be cut in half to serve four people. A large tagine with a deep bottom works best for this recipe.

● **Large tagine**

¼ cup	all-purpose flour	60 mL
1 tbsp	Bahrat Spice Blend (page 39) or store-bought garam masala	15 mL
1 lb	cubed stewing beef	500 g
3 tbsp	avocado or olive oil	45 mL
1	onion, cut into quarters	1
1	red bell pepper, chopped	1
1	leek, white and tender green parts, sliced	1
6	cloves garlic, crushed	6
1	can (28 oz/796 mL) diced tomatoes with juice	1
1	medium zucchini, chopped	1
2 cups	chopped fennel bulb or cabbage	500 mL

1. In a bowl, combine flour and spice blend. Add beef cubes and toss well to coat. Set aside.

2. In the bottom of a flameproof tagine, heat oil over medium heat. Add onion, bell pepper and leek and cook, stirring, for 15 minutes or until soft and slightly colored. Add garlic and stewing beef, scraping loose flour mixture into the tagine bottom. Cook, stirring constantly, for 3 to 5 minutes or until flour is slightly browned.

3. Add tomatoes with juice, zucchini and fennel and bring to a boil, stirring frequently. Cover with tagine lid, reduce heat to low and simmer, stirring occasionally, for 1 to 1½ hours. Beef should cut easily with a fork and if not quite tender, replace cover and cook until beef is tender.

Beef Tagine with Coriander and Quince

Makes 4 to 6 servings

Sweet-sour tagine dishes are a direct descendant of ancient Persian cuisine, and the quince adds the tart spike in this recipe. The method used is slightly different in this recipe as well, reflecting the traditional method of nomadic Berbers. Coriander is used in this dish in both the Bahrat spice blend and the fresh cilantro leaves.

Tip

If you are replacing the quince with pear or apple, reduce the amount of honey in the recipe and pass honey at the table for those who wish to add it.

● **Medium or large tagine**

1½ lbs	cubed stewing beef	750 g
1	onion, coarsely chopped	1
1 tbsp	Bahrat Spice Blend (page 39) or store-bought garam masala	15 mL
1 tbsp	grated fresh gingerroot	15 mL
¼ cup	chopped fresh cilantro, divided	60 mL
1 cup	beef broth	250 mL
¼ cup	red wine	60 mL
1 tbsp	butter or toasted sesame oil	15 mL
4	quinces or pears, cut into quarters	4
1 cup	chopped prunes	250 mL
2 tbsp	liquid honey	30 mL

1. In the bottom of a flameproof tagine, combine stewing beef, onion, spice blend, ginger, 2 tbsp (30 mL) of the cilantro, broth and wine. Bring to a boil over medium heat. Cover with tagine lid, reduce heat to low and simmer, stirring occasionally, for 45 minutes.

2. Stir in butter until incorporated. Add quinces, prunes and honey. Replace lid and cook for 20 to 30 minutes. Beef should cut easily with a fork and if not quite tender, replace cover and cook until beef is tender. Garnish with remaining cilantro.

Beef Tagine with Figs and Walnuts

Makes 4 to 6 servings

Fresh figs have been cultivated in the Mediterranean region for thousands of years and are sold in the Moroccan souk along with spices and other exotic fruits. Available from June through September, fresh figs are sweet, soft and chewy. Use them in tagine recipes whenever they are available.

Tip

Figs arrived in Florida with Spanish explorers in around 1575 and "Mission" figs were planted by Spanish Franciscan missionaries in California in the 18th century. Now California produces 20 percent of the world's dried figs.

● **Medium or large tagine**

3 tbsp	avocado or olive oil	45 mL
2	onions, cut into quarters	2
1 tbsp	La Kama Spice Blend (page 44)	15 mL
½ tsp	ground cinnamon	2 mL
1½ lbs	cubed stewing beef	750 g
1 cup	beef broth	250 mL
¼ cup	ground walnuts or almonds	60 mL
1 tbsp	Pomegranate Molasses (page 172) or store-bought	15 mL
1 cup	chopped fresh or dried figs (see Tip, left)	250 mL
1 cup	walnut halves	250 mL

1. In the bottom of a flameproof tagine, heat oil over medium heat. Add onions, spice blend and cinnamon and cook, stirring, for 5 minutes. Add beef, stirring to coat beef with vegetables and seasonings. Cook, stirring occasionally, for 7 to 10 minutes or until beef is browned on all sides.

2. Add broth, ground walnuts and pomegranate molasses. Bring to a boil. Cover with tagine lid, reduce heat to low and simmer, stirring occasionally, for 45 minutes. Add figs, replace lid and simmer for 15 to 20 minutes. Beef should cut easily with a fork and if not quite tender, replace cover and simmer until beef is tender. Toss walnut halves into the tagine and serve.

Beef Tagine with Okra and Tomatoes

Makes 4 to 6 servings

Fresh okra is available in North America at farmers' markets and some supermarkets in the late summer and early fall. Some like it cooked whole, on top of the tagine, but I prefer to chop the okra and add it to the dish earlier in the cooking process so that it melts into the stew, thickening it as it cooks.

Tips

Look for small, firm okra pods that are slightly sticky to the touch. Fresh is best, but frozen okra may be substituted if fresh is not available.

If you wish to cook okra whole, add it to the tagine with date molasses in Step 2, replace the lid and simmer for 20 to 30 minutes or until okra is tender. You may need to add up to ¼ cup (60 mL) tomato juice or water if the tagine seems a bit dry to provide enough steam to cook the okra.

● **Medium or large tagine**

3 tbsp	avocado or olive oil	45 mL
1	onion, cut into quarters	1
1 tbsp	Moroccan Cinnamon Spice Blend (page 47) or store-bought garam masala	15 mL
1½ lbs	cubed stewing beef	750 g
3	cloves garlic, finely chopped	3
1	can (28 oz/796 mL) diced tomatoes with juice	1
18 to 20	small fresh okra (about 1 lb/500 g), chopped, or 1 medium zucchini, chopped (see Tips, left)	18 to 20
2 tbsp	Date Molasses (page 170) or honey	30 mL

1. In the bottom of a flameproof tagine, heat oil over medium heat. Add onion and spice blend and cook, stirring, for 5 minutes. Add beef and garlic, stirring to coat beef with onion and seasonings. Cook, stirring occasionally, for 7 to 10 minutes or until beef is browned on all sides.

2. Add tomatoes with juice and okra. Bring to a boil. Cover with tagine lid, reduce heat to low and simmer, stirring occasionally, for 1 hour. Add molasses, replace lid and simmer for 10 to 15 minutes. Beef should cut easily with a fork and if not quite tender, replace cover and simmer until beef is tender.

Beef Tagine with Peaches and Raisins

Makes 4 to 6 servings

Peaches sweeten the beef tagine and, if added at the end of the cooking time, stay intact. Sometimes I substitute canned pineapple chunks for the peaches and add one tablespoon (15 mL) extra wine vinegar to maintain the sweet-sour balance.

Tip

You can toast nuts and seeds in the bottom of a nonstick coated tagine over medium heat, stirring constantly, for 1 to 2 minutes, until lightly colored. Tip into a bowl and reserve until called for in the recipe.

● **Medium or large tagine**

1½ lbs	cubed stewing beef	750 g
¼ cup	Chermoula Moroccan Rub (page 40)	60 mL
3 tbsp	all-purpose flour	45 mL
3 tbsp	warm water	45 mL
20	threads saffron	20
3 tbsp	avocado or olive oil	45 mL
1	onion, cut in half and sliced	1
½ cup	beef broth or reserved peach juice	125 mL
3 tbsp	red wine vinegar	45 mL
½ cup	raisins	125 mL
4	fresh peaches, sliced, or 1 can (14 oz/398 mL) sliced peaches, juice reserved	4
3 tbsp	toasted sesame seeds (see Tip, left)	45 mL

1. In a bowl, toss beef with spice rub and flour until coated. Set aside. In a separate bowl, combine water and saffron threads and set aside.

2. In the bottom of a flameproof tagine, heat oil over medium heat. Add onion and cook, stirring, for 5 minutes. Add beef, scraping loose flour and spice mixture into the tagine bottom. Cook, stirring constantly, for 3 to 5 minutes or until flour is slightly browned.

3. Add broth, vinegar, and saffron and soaking water. Bring to a boil. Cover with tagine lid, reduce heat to low and simmer, stirring occasionally, for 1 hour. Add raisins and peach slices, replace lid and simmer for 15 to 20 minutes. Beef should cut easily with a fork and if not quite tender, replace cover and simmer until beef is tender. Garnish with sesame seeds.

Beef Tagine with Squash and Beets

Makes 4 to 6 servings

Rustic and hearty, this warming winter tagine uses ginger and hot chile pepper for a touch of spicy heat.

Tip

I recommend the use of organic, cold-pressed extra virgin avocado oil in the tagine recipes in this book because it is excellent for medium to high heat cooking. Unlike other polyunsaturated oils, olive oil in particular, avocado oil does not break down under high heat cooking. It is an excellent source of vitamin E and contains beneficial omega-3, 6 and 9 fatty acids.

● **Medium or large tagine**

3 tbsp	avocado or olive oil	45 mL
1	onion, cut in half and sliced	1
1 tbsp	Ras el Hanout (page 50) or hot sauce	15 mL
1 lb	cubed stewing beef	500 g
4	cloves garlic, crushed	4
1	hot chile pepper, chopped, or 1 dried cayenne pepper, crushed	1
1	slice candied ginger, chopped	1
4	medium beets, quartered	4
2 cups	diced squash	500 mL
1 cup	beef broth	250 mL
2	oranges, cut into segments	2
2 cups	fresh or frozen chopped Swiss chard	500 mL
½ cup	chopped fresh cilantro or flat-leaf parsley	125 mL

1. In the bottom of a flameproof tagine, heat oil over medium heat. Add onion and ras el hanout and cook, stirring, for 5 minutes. Add beef, garlic, chile pepper and ginger, stirring well to coat beef with vegetables and seasonings. Cook, stirring occasionally, for 7 to 10 minutes or until beef is browned on all sides.

2. Add beets, squash and broth and bring to a boil, stirring occasionally. Cover with tagine lid, reduce heat to low and simmer, stirring occasionally, for 45 minutes. Add oranges and Swiss chard, replace lid and cook for 15 to 20 minutes. Beef should cut easily with a fork and if not quite tender, replace cover and cook until beef is tender. Garnish with parsley.

Fiery Beef Tagine with Vegetables

Makes 4 to 6 servings

Harissa is used with the Berbere spice blend in this tagine for a spicy-hot dish. Yogurt is added as a cooling garnish for the dish, but you can reduce the amount of harissa added in order to control the heat or omit it completely and serve the harissa separately at the table.

● **Medium tagine**

3 tbsp	avocado or olive oil	45 mL
1	onion, coarsely chopped	1
½	red or green bell pepper, chopped	½
1	slice candied ginger, chopped	1
1 tbsp	Harissa (page 45) or hot pepper sauce	15 mL
2 tsp	Berbere (page 42) or store-bought garam masala	10 mL
1 lb	cubed stewing beef, cut into cubes	500 g
3	tomatoes, peeled and quartered (about 8 oz/250 g)	3
1	Preserved Lemon or Frozen Lemon (pages 48 and 49), shredded or finely chopped	1
2 cups	diced squash	500 mL
2 cups	fresh or frozen green peas	500 mL
2 cups	Balkan-style yogurt	500 mL
½ cup	chopped fresh cilantro or flat-leaf parsley	125 mL

1. In the bottom of a flameproof tagine, heat oil over medium heat. Add onion and bell pepper and cook, stirring, for 5 minutes. Add ginger, Harissa, Berbere and stewing beef, stirring well to coat beef with vegetables and seasonings. Cook, stirring occasionally, for 7 to 10 minutes or until beef is browned on all sides.

2. Add tomatoes, lemon rind, flesh and any juices, and squash and bring to a boil, stirring occasionally. Cover with tagine lid, reduce heat to low and simmer, stirring occasionally, for 45 minutes. Add peas, replace lid and cook for 10 to 15 minutes. Beef should cut easily with a fork and if not quite tender, replace cover and cook until beef is tender. Garnish with yogurt and cilantro.

Gingered Beef Tagine with Tomato Sauce

Makes 4 to 6 servings

Easy, fast and fresh tasting with a homemade tomato sauce, this dish is a great fall entrée when tomatoes are flooding the markets.

Tips

Candied ginger is sold in 1-inch (2.5 cm) crosswise slices or cubes, widely available in supermarkets and specialty food stores. Use 1 tbsp (15 mL) grated fresh gingerroot in place of the candied ginger.

In winter, substitute 1 can (14 oz/398 mL) drained tomatoes for the fresh tomatoes.

● **Medium tagine**

3 tbsp	avocado or olive oil	45 mL
1	onion, coarsely chopped	1
1	red bell pepper, chopped	1
4	cloves garlic, coarsely chopped	4
1	slice candied ginger, chopped (see Tips, left)	1
1 tbsp	Bahrat Spice Blend (page 39) or store-bought garam masala	15 mL
1/4 tsp	ground nutmeg	1 mL
1 lb	cubed stewing beef	500 g
3	tomatoes, peeled and quartered (about 8 oz/250 g) (see Tips, left)	3
1	medium zucchini, chopped	1
1/4 cup	sesame seeds	60 mL

1. In the bottom of a flameproof tagine, heat oil over medium heat. Add onion and bell pepper and cook, stirring, for 5 minutes. Add garlic, ginger, spice blend, nutmeg and stewing beef, stirring well to coat beef with vegetables and seasonings. Cook, stirring occasionally, for 7 to 10 minutes or until beef is browned on all sides.

2. Add tomatoes and zucchini and bring to a boil, stirring occasionally. Cover with tagine lid, reduce heat to low and simmer, stirring occasionally, for 45 minutes. Beef should cut easily with a fork and if not quite tender, replace cover and simmer until beef is tender. Garnish with sesame seeds.

Ground Beef and Root Vegetable Tagine

**Makes
4 servings**

Ground beef is faster cooking, making this tagine a weekday winner. Use almost any vegetable, such as broccoli, cauliflower, Brussels sprouts, cabbage or turnips in this warming winter stew.

● **Medium tagine**

2 tbsp	avocado or olive oil	30 mL
1	onion, coarsely chopped	1
½	red or green bell pepper, chopped	½
1 lb	lean ground beef	500 g
½ tsp	ground nutmeg	2 mL
1 cup	beef broth, divided	250 mL
	Juice of ½ fresh lemon or Frozen Lemon (page 49)	
2 cups	diced rutabaga	500 mL
2	carrots, chopped	2
2	parsnips, chopped	2
3 tbsp	all-purpose flour	45 mL
1 tbsp	Berbere (page 42) or store-bought garam masala	15 mL
½ cup	chopped fresh flat-leaf parsley	125 mL

1. In the bottom of a flameproof tagine, heat oil over medium heat. Add onion and bell pepper and cook, stirring, for 5 minutes. Add ground beef and nutmeg. Cook, stirring and breaking up clumps of meat with the back of a spoon, for 7 to 10 minutes or until beef is lightly browned and no longer pink inside.

2. Add ¾ cup (175 mL) of the broth and lemon juice and bring to a boil, stirring occasionally. Stir in rutabaga, carrots and parsnips. Cover with tagine lid, reduce heat to low and simmer, stirring occasionally, for 15 minutes.

3. Meanwhile, in a bowl, combine flour and Berbere. Stir in remaining broth until mixture reaches a smooth paste. Stir flour mixture into tagine, replace lid and cook, stirring frequently, for 10 to 15 minutes or until sauce is thickened and vegetables are tender. Garnish with parsley.

Spiced Kefta in Tomato Sauce

Makes 4 to 6 servings

Kefta (or Kofta) is the North African name for chopped or minced meat, usually beef or lamb, but sometimes chicken, that is formed into balls and poached in a tangy sauce.

Tips

You can purchase low-fat beef (or chicken) meatballs and use them with the sauce to save time. Or you can make a large quantity of homemade meatballs (you can double the recipe for Kefta, right) and freeze them for convenience. If you add frozen meatballs to the hot sauce, allow an extra 10 to 15 minutes for thawing and heating them through.

Instead of chopped hot chile pepper, use 1 crushed dried cayenne pepper.

In winter, substitute 1 can (14 oz/398 mL) drained tomatoes for the fresh tomatoes.

- **Baking sheet, lined with parchment or waxed paper**
- **Medium or large tagine**

Kefta (meatballs)

1 lb	ground lean beef, lamb or chicken	500 g
½ cup	fresh bread crumbs	125 mL
½	onion, finely chopped	½
2	cloves garlic, minced	2
1 tbsp	Berbere (page 42)	15 mL
1	egg	1
½ tsp	sea salt	2 mL

Tomato Sauce

2 tbsp	avocado or olive oil	30 mL
1	onion, coarsely chopped	1
1 tbsp	Ras el Hanout (page 50) or store-bought	15 mL
4	cloves garlic, coarsely chopped	4
1	hot chile pepper, chopped, (see Tips, left)	1
1 tbsp	grated fresh gingerroot	15 mL
4	tomatoes, peeled and quartered (about 12 oz/375 g) (see Tips, left)	4
	Juice of 1 fresh lemon or Frozen Lemon (page 49)	
	Flesh and rind of ½ Preserved Lemon or Frozen Lemon (pages 48 and 49), finely chopped, optional	
2 cups	chopped fresh or frozen spinach	500 mL

1. *Meatballs:* In a bowl, combine beef, bread crumbs, onion, garlic, Berbere, egg and salt. Mix well using your hands. Scoop out 2 tbsp (30 mL) of beef mixture and roll into meatballs between the palms of your hands. Place on prepared baking sheet. Use immediately or flash freeze on baking sheet in the coldest part of the freezer. Transfer to an airtight container, label and keep frozen for up to 3 months.

2. *Sauce:* In the bottom of a flameproof tagine, heat oil over medium heat. Add onion and ras el hanout and cook, stirring, for 5 minutes. Add garlic, chile and ginger and cook, stirring, for 5 to 7 minutes or until vegetables are soft. Add tomatoes, lemon juice, and flesh and rind, if using, and bring to a boil. Reduce heat and simmer, stirring occasionally, uncovered, for 10 minutes or until sauce thickens slightly.

3. Stir in spinach and simmer for about 5 minutes or until spinach is wilted and sauce is simmering. Using tongs, place the keftas in the sauce. Cover, reduce heat to low and simmer, gently turning the meatballs 3 or 4 times during cooking, for 15 to 20 minutes. Cut a meatball in half to check that the meat is cooked all the way through (there should be no sign of pink) and if not, simmer until meatballs are cooked through.

Hot Paprika Beef Tagine

Makes 4 servings

Hot paprika is powdered dried hot chile peppers as opposed to the sweet red bell peppers used in the paprika that North Americans are most familiar with. Depending on the hot peppers used in the paprika, it ranges from mild to fiery hot.

Tip
You can purchase hot paprika at a Middle Eastern food store or mix your own blend consisting of equal parts sweet paprika with ground chile peppers.

● **Medium tagine**

2 tbsp	avocado or olive oil	30 mL
1	onion, cut into quarters	1
1	red bell pepper, chopped	1
2 tsp	hot paprika (see Tip, left)	10 mL
1 tsp	ground coriander	5 mL
½ tsp	ground cinnamon	2 mL
1 lb	cubed stewing beef	500 g
3	cloves garlic, finely chopped	3
½ cup	beef broth	125 mL
3	carrots, cut lengthwise into quarters	3
8	pitted prunes, cut lengthwise into quarters	8

1. In the bottom of a flameproof tagine, heat oil over medium heat. Add onion, bell pepper, paprika, coriander and cinnamon and cook, stirring, for 5 minutes. Add beef and garlic and cook, stirring frequently, for 7 to 10 minutes or until beef is lightly browned on all sides.

2. Add broth, carrots and prunes and bring liquids to a boil, stirring occasionally. Cover with tagine lid, reduce heat to low and simmer, stirring occasionally, for 1 hour. Beef should cut easily with a fork and if not quite tender, replace cover and simmer until beef is tender.

Spiced Honey Lemon Beef Tagine

Makes 4 to 6 servings

Pomegranate molasses and preserved lemon provide the tang as a balance to the honey in this dish.

● **Medium or large tagine**

3 tbsp	liquid honey	45 mL
1 tbsp	toasted sesame oil	15 mL
1 tsp	Pomegranate Molasses (page 172) or store-bought	5 mL
3	cloves garlic, minced	3
1 tbsp	Ras el Hanout (page 50) or store-bought	15 mL
1 lb	cubed stewing beef	500 g
2 tbsp	avocado or olive oil	30 mL
1	onion, cut into quarters	1
1	red bell pepper, chopped	1
½ cup	beef broth	125 mL
	Juice of 1 fresh lemon or Frozen Lemon (page 49)	
	Flesh and rind of ½ Preserved Lemon or Frozen Lemon (pages 48 and 49), chopped	
3	parsnips, chopped	3

1. In a bowl, combine honey, sesame oil, molasses, garlic and ras el hanout. Toss beef in the mixture and set aside for up to 30 minutes or cover and refrigerate for up to 24 hours. Let meat return to room temperature before cooking.

2. In the bottom of a flameproof tagine, heat oil over medium heat. Add onion and bell pepper and cook, stirring, for 5 minutes. Add beef broth and lemon juice, flesh and rind and bring to a boil. Stir in parsnips and beef with marinade until honey is dissolved. Cover with tagine lid, reduce heat to low and simmer, stirring occasionally, for 1 hour. Beef should cut easily with a fork and if not quite tender, replace cover and simmer until beef is tender.

Fish and Seafood

Almond Whitefish with Broccoli and Dates

Makes 4 servings

I particularly like the subtle sweetness of this sauce with the toasted nuts.

Tips

Mullet is very nice in this dish but you can use other white fish fillets such as haddock, black sea bass, catfish or Pacific halibut.

Note that there is a range of weight suggested for the fish because of the wide range in tagine sizes. You will need to purchase 4 large or smaller fillets depending on the size of your tagine.

Once the fish is cooked, remove skin using a paring knife. It will slip easily away from the flesh.

● **Medium tagine**

2 tbsp	butter	30 mL
1 cup	almond slivers	250 mL
2 tbsp	avocado or olive oil	30 mL
1 tbsp	Ras el Hanout (page 50) or store-bought	15 mL
½	fennel bulb, chopped	½
½ cup	chicken broth or fish stock	125 mL
	Juice of ½ fresh lemon or Frozen Lemon (page 49)	
¼ cup	chopped dates	60 mL
2 cups	sliced broccoli florets	500 mL
4	mullet or other whitefish fillets, skin on one side (approximately 1 to 1½ lbs/500 to 750 g) (see Tips, left)	4

1. In the bottom of a flameproof tagine, melt butter over medium heat. Add almond slivers and cook, stirring, for 3 to 5 minutes or just until lightly colored. Using a slotted spoon, lift out into a bowl and set aside.

2. Add oil to same tagine bottom and heat over medium heat. Stir in ras el hanout and fennel and cook, stirring, for 5 minutes. Add broth, lemon juice and dates and bring to a boil. Add broccoli and cook, stirring frequently, for 5 minutes. Lay fish on top of vegetables, skin side up. Cover with tagine lid, reduce heat to low and simmer for 15 to 20 minutes or until fish turns opaque and flakes easily with a fork. Garnish with almonds and season to taste at the table.

Artichoke and Shellfish in Almond Milk

Makes 4 to 6 servings

This is such a stunning dish that it makes the perfect entrée for entertaining. If you cook the mussels and shrimp ahead of time, the whole dish can be on the table in less than 30 minutes.

Tip

Serve with flatbread or rice, noodles or couscous.

● **Medium or large tagine**

2 tbsp	avocado or olive oil	30 mL
1 tbsp	butter	15 mL
4	shallots, chopped	4
½	fennel bulb, chopped	½
2	cloves garlic, chopped	2
2 tsp	Moroccan Cinnamon Spice Blend (page 47) or Ras el Hanout (page 50)	10 mL
¼ cup	almond, rice or coconut milk	60 mL
1 lb	mussels, scrubbed and debearded	500 g
1 lb	shrimp, shells on, rinsed	500 g
	Juice of ½ fresh lemon	
1	jar (6 oz/175 mL) marinated quartered artichoke hearts, drained	1
¼ cup	heavy or whipping (35%) cream	60 mL
½ cup	chopped fresh cilantro or flat-leaf parsley	125 mL

1. In bottom of flameproof tagine, heat oil and melt butter over medium heat. Add shallots, fennel, garlic and spice blend and cook, stirring, for 5 minutes. Add almond milk and stir well. Cover with tagine lid, reduce heat to low and cook for 12 minutes without lifting the lid.

2. Meanwhile, combine mussels, shrimp and lemon juice in a saucepan and add just enough water to cover. Bring liquids to a simmer over medium-high heat and simmer gently for 2 to 3 minutes or until shrimp turn bright pink and most of the mussel shells open. Using a colander or sieve, drain and rinse under cool water. Discard any mussels that have not opened. Remove shells from shrimp and mussels, leaving shells on a few mussels for a dramatic effect, if desired.

3. Stir artichoke hearts, mussels, shrimp and cream into vegetables in tagine. Cook, stirring, over low to medium-low heat for 2 to 3 minutes or until sauce is bubbly and shellfish is heated through. Garnish with cilantro just before serving.

Baked Fish Tagine

**Makes
4 servings**

The source of this recipe is from ancient times when sardines were layered in traditional clay tagines with fresh green herbs and onions, drizzled with oil and set into fires to sizzle and bake. Still popular today, this tagine is changed only by the addition of tomatoes.

Tip

Sardines are the fish of choice for this dish, but other fresh oily fish such as salmon, trout, anchovy, smelt and mackerel may be substituted if fresh sardines are not available.

- **Medium tagine**
- **Preheat oven to 375°F (190°C)**

2	onions, chopped	2
¼	fennel bulb, chopped	¼
¼ cup	Chermoula Moroccan Rub (page 40)	60 mL
1	can (14 oz/398 mL) diced tomatoes with juice	1
1 lb	sardine fillets (see Tip, left)	500 g
2 tbsp	avocado or olive oil	30 mL

1. In a large bowl, combine onions, fennel and spice rub. Set aside.

2. Spoon one-third of the tomatoes with juice into the bottom of a tagine. Layer half of the sardine fillets over tomatoes and top with half of the onion mixture. Drizzle 1 tbsp (15 mL) oil over all. Repeat layers, finishing with remaining tomatoes.

3. Bake in preheated oven for 20 to 30 minutes or until fish flakes easily with a fork.

Black Cod in Chermoula Sauce

Makes 4 to 6 servings

Black cod is firm in texture with large, velvety flakes that are plump with a sweet, rich flavor. It is a good variety for cooking in a tagine because it does not lose its texture.

Tip

Because of concerns about the environmental sustainability of some fish and seafood, we recommend that you check reliable sites such as www.montereybayaquarium.org or www.seachoice.org for the latest information on fish before purchasing.

Variation

You can substitute snapper for black cod in this recipe.

● **Medium or large tagine**

3 tbsp	all-purpose flour	45 mL
1 tsp	sweet paprika	5 mL
½ tsp	ground cumin	2 mL
½ tsp	ground coriander	2 mL
1½ lbs	black cod fillets	750 g
¼ cup	Chermoula Moroccan Rub (page 40) or chili sauce	60 mL
3 tbsp	avocado or olive oil	45 mL
2	onions, cut in half and sliced	2
3	cloves garlic, sliced	3
1	can (14 oz/398 mL) diced tomatoes with juice	1

1. In a large bowl, combine flour, paprika, cumin and coriander. Cut fish into 1-inch (2.5 cm) cubes and drop into flour, tossing to coat. Lift out and set fish in a shallow dish. Discard remaining seasoned flour. Toss chermoula rub with fish to coat. Set aside.

2. In the bottom of a flameproof tagine, heat oil over medium heat. Add onions and garlic and cook, stirring, for 7 to 12 minutes or until soft. Add tomatoes with juice and fish and bring to a gentle simmer. Cover, reduce heat to low and simmer gently for 15 to 20 minutes or until fish is opaque and flakes easily with a fork.

Fish and Chickpeas with Pomegranate and Roasted Red Peppers

Makes 4 to 6 servings

The tart-sweet pomegranate molasses combines well with the nutty, rich taste of the roasted peppers for a delightful sauce.

Tips

Roasting red peppers is not difficult (see page 51) and I try to make extra and freeze them, but when I run out of my own stash, I have found some very good commercial canned red peppers for my pantry.

Use a medium to firm-textured fish such as haddock, catfish, Pacific halibut, snapper, black sea bass or trout in this dish.

● **Medium or large tagine**

3 tbsp	avocado or olive oil	45 mL
2	onions, cut in half and sliced	2
3	cloves garlic, sliced	3
2 tbsp	La Kama Spice Blend (page 44) or steak seasoning	30 mL
1	can (14 to 19 oz/398 to 540 mL) chickpeas, drained and rinsed	1
¼ cup	chicken broth	60 mL
2 tbsp	Pomegranate Molasses (page 172) or store-bought	30 mL
2	Roasted Red Peppers (page 51), cut into strips (see Tips, left)	2
1½ lbs	skinless firm whitefish fillets (see Tips, left)	750 g
¼ cup	pomegranate seeds, optional	60 mL

1. In the bottom of a flameproof tagine, heat oil over medium heat. Add onions and garlic and cook, stirring, for 7 to 12 minutes or until soft. Add spice blend and chickpeas and cook, stirring constantly, for 1 minute to coat chickpeas. Add broth and molasses and bring to a gentle simmer. Stir in roasted peppers and lay fish fillets over top. Cover, reduce heat to low and simmer gently for 15 to 20 minutes or until fish is opaque and flakes easily with a fork. Garnish with pomegranate seeds, if using.

Whitefish in Spinach Sauce

**Makes
4 servings**

Surprisingly easy and
very fast, this dish works
for weekday dinners but
is impressive enough for
company. Fresh whitefish,
such as catfish or cod,
work well in this recipe
because their firm texture
holds together with the
spinach. Use fresh fish and
fresh spinach whenever
possible.

Tips

A 12-oz (375 g) package of
fresh spinach yields 6 cups
(1.5 L) spinach, which is ideal,
but you can use an 8- or
10-ounce package (250 or
300 g) in the sauce with
good results.

To Drain Yogurt: Set a
stainless-steel strainer or
colander over a bowl large
enough to hold 2 cups
(500 mL) of liquid. Line the
strainer with a double layer of
clean cheesecloth. Pour 2 cups
(500 mL) of fresh plain yogurt
into the lined strainer and
cover the strainer with plastic
wrap or fold up the edges of
the cheesecloth to enclose the
top of the yogurt. Set the bowl
and strainer in the refrigerator
and let the watery whey drain
away from the yogurt solids for
10 minutes. The yogurt will be
thick and creamy but with a
soft yogurt texture.

● **Medium tagine**

2 tbsp	avocado or olive oil	30 mL
1	onion, chopped	1
1 tbsp	Fennel Seasoning (page 43) or fennel seeds	15 mL
4	fresh fish fillets (about 1½ lbs/750 g)	4
	Sea salt and freshly ground black pepper	
¼ to ½ cup	water	60 to 125 mL
2 tbsp	freshly squeezed lemon juice	30 mL
6 cups	packed coarsely chopped spinach leaves (see Tips, left)	1.5 L
⅔ cup	Drained Yogurt (see Tips, left)	150 mL

1. In the bottom of a flameproof tagine, heat oil over
   medium heat. Add onion and seasoning and cook,
   stirring, for 5 minutes. Add fish to tagine and season
   with salt and pepper. Add water and lemon juice so
   that water is slightly more than halfway over fish.
   Bring to a gentle simmer over medium-low heat.
   Cover, reduce heat to low and gently simmer, turning
   fish once, for 10 minutes or until fish is opaque and
   flakes easily with a fork.

2. Transfer fish to a platter and keep warm. Add
   spinach to tagine and cook over medium heat for 2 to
   3 minutes or until wilted and liquid has evaporated.
   Drain excess liquid if the spinach is cooked before it is
   all evaporated. Stir in yogurt. Return fish to the sauce
   and heat through.

Fish Cakes in Spiced Tomato Sauce

Makes 4 servings

The flavor and color of saffron is evident in the delicate fish cakes, and the raisins sweeten the tagine. Raw fish is blended to a paste and formed into bite-size balls (or mini "cakes"), which are gently simmered in a Moroccan-flavored tomato sauce. For convenience, make double the amount of fish cakes and freeze the extra.

- Medium tagine
- Rimmed baking sheet, lined with waxed or parchment paper

Fish Cakes

¼ cup	sultana raisins (see Tips, right)	60 mL
20	saffron threads	20
3 tbsp	tomato paste	45 mL
¼ cup	warm water	60 mL
1 lb	skinless whitefish fillets, cut into chunks (see Tips, right)	500 g
2	green onions, coarsely chopped	2
2	sprigs flat-leaf parsley or cilantro	2
½ cup	fresh bread crumbs	125 mL
½ tsp	salt	2 mL
1	egg	1

Tomato Sauce

3 tbsp	avocado or olive oil	45 mL
2	onions, cut in half and sliced	2
3	cloves garlic, chopped	3
1 cup	sliced mushrooms	250 mL
2 tsp	sweet paprika	10 mL
½ to 1 tsp	Harissa (page 45) or chile powder	2 to 5 mL
1	can (28 oz/796 mL) whole tomatoes with juice	1

1. *Fish Cakes:* In a bowl, combine raisins, saffron, tomato paste and water. Set aside.

2. In a food processor, process fish chunks, green onions, parsley, bread crumbs and salt until finely chopped. Add egg and saffron mixture and process until blended to a stiff, thick paste. If too dry to hold together, add warm water by the tablespoon (15 mL) with motor running through opening in the feed tube to form a stiff, thick paste. If too thin, stir in dry bread crumbs by the tablespoon (15 mL) until mixture holds together in a stiff, thick paste.

Sultana raisins are golden in color and are the preferred type for the fish cakes.

A medium to firm-textured fish, such as haddock, cod, catfish, Pacific halibut, snapper, black sea bass or turbot, is the best variety for forming the fish cakes.

3. Use a tablespoon (15 mL) to scoop fish mixture and shape into cakes with your hands. Use immediately or place on prepared baking sheet, cover with plastic wrap and refrigerate for up to 12 hours. Cakes may be flash frozen on the baking sheet, transferred to a freezer container and stored for up to 2 months. Bring to room temperature (or thaw) before cooking in tomato sauce.

4. *Tomato Sauce:* In the bottom of a flameproof tagine, heat oil over medium heat. Add onions and cook, stirring, for 5 minutes. Add garlic, mushrooms, paprika and harissa and cook, stirring occasionally, for 5 to 7 minutes or until vegetables are soft. Add tomatoes with juice and fish cakes and bring to a gentle simmer. Cover with tagine lid, reduce heat to low and simmer gently, stirring once, for 20 to 30 minutes or until fish cakes have turned opaque throughout.

Sea Bream in Sesame Sauce

Makes 4 servings

Sesame adds its nutty flavor to the delicate taste of the medium-fleshed sea bream in this simple dish.

Tips

If you can't find sea bream, use Pacific halibut or black sea bass.

Because of concerns about the environmental sustainability of some fish and seafood, we recommend that you check reliable sites such as www.montereybayaquarium. org or www.seachoice.org for the latest information on fish before purchasing.

● **Medium tagine**

2 tbsp	avocado zest or olive oil	30 mL
1	onion, cut in half and sliced	1
2 tsp	Za'atar (page 54) or dried oregano	10 mL
1	can (19 oz/540 mL) whole tomatoes, drained	1
½ cup	Sesame Mayonnaise (page 158)	125 mL
1 to 1½ lbs	sea bream fillets, skin on one side (see Tips, left, and page 112)	500 to 750 g

1. In the bottom of a flameproof tagine, heat oil over medium heat. Add onion and cook, stirring, for 5 minutes. Add za'atar, tomatoes and Sesame Mayonnaise and bring to a boil. Lay fish in the sauce, skin side up. Cover with tagine lid, reduce heat to low and simmer gently for 15 to 20 minutes or until fish is opaque and flakes easily with a fork.

Fruited Salmon with Mushrooms and Mustard Sauce

Makes 4 servings

This is perhaps my favorite dish. The tangy mustard sauce is rich in flavor and best of all, it is fast and easy. I use seasonal tree fruit — apricots in spring, peaches and plums in summer and pears in fall and winter. This way I can enjoy it all year.

Tips

Once the fish is cooked, remove skin using a paring knife. It will slip easily away from the flesh.

Sometimes it is difficult to purchase fish to the exact weight, therefore I have given a range. The important thing to remember when purchasing ingredients for tagine cooking is to know the capacity of your own tagine.

● Medium tagine

2 tbsp	avocado or olive oil	30 mL
1	onion, cut in half and sliced	1
4	cloves garlic, sliced	4
1 tbsp	butter	15 mL
4 cups	quartered mushrooms	1 L
1	pear, chopped	1
½	Preserved Lemon or Frozen Lemon (pages 48 and 49), finely chopped	½
1 tbsp	whole-grain Dijon mustard	15 mL
1 to 1½ lbs	salmon fillet, skin on one side (see Tips, left)	500 to 750 g

1. In the bottom of a flameproof tagine, heat oil over medium heat. Add onion and cook, stirring, for 5 minutes. Add garlic, butter and mushrooms and cook, stirring frequently, for 5 to 7 minutes or until mushrooms begin to soften. Stir in pear, flesh with juice of lemon and mustard and cook, stirring constantly, for 1 minute. Lay salmon over vegetables, skin side up. Cover with tagine lid and cook for 15 to 20 minutes or until fish turns opaque and flakes easily with a fork.

Chicken with Dried Fruit and Peppers (page 61)

Golden Chicken with Potatoes and Chickpeas (page 66)

Cinnamon Lamb Tagine with Apricots (page 80)

Lamb Tagine with Oranges
and Dates (page 90)

Beef, Leek and Onion Tagine (page 99)

Beef Tagine with Squash and Beets (page 104)

Fish and Chickpeas with Pomegranate
and Roasted Red Peppers (page 116)

Fruits de Mer (page 121)

Fennel, Artichoke and Potato Tagine (page 139)

Lentil and Almond
Tagine (page 141)

Herbed Feta Dip (page 155)

Hot and Spicy Chickpeas and Almonds (page 166)

Moroccan Sweet Potato Soup (page 182)

Beet and Feta Cheese Salad (page 191)

Green Bean, Pistachio and Pomegranate Salad (page 196)

Gingered Fruit Tagine (page 210)

Fruits de Mer

Makes 6 servings

All around the Mediterranean, fish and shellfish are combined in ways that reflect the culture of the sea and the people of the coastal regions. For North Africans, this is a festive dish reserved for celebrations. It is a riot of color and rich in the flavors of Morocco, so do not be surprised at the long list of ingredients. Once the ingredients are assembled, it is remarkably easy and fast to make. Serve this with lightly buttered couscous and celebrate.

Tip

Traditional Berber tagines featured lamb, goat meat or vegetables most often, with fowl occasionally. Fish and shellfish are a modern adaptation found in Moroccan restaurants in the tourist areas of Casablanca, Fez and Tangier.

● **Large tagine**

3 tbsp	avocado or olive oil	45 mL
6	cloves garlic, finely sliced	6
1 tbsp	Berbere (page 42) or store-bought garam masala	15 mL
2	carrots, cut into matchsticks	2
2	parsnips, cut into matchsticks	2
1	zucchini, cut into matchsticks	1
1	onion, cut in half and sliced	1
½	red bell pepper, cut into thin strips	½
½	green bell pepper, cut into thin strips	½
1 cup	fish stock or chicken broth	250 mL
½ cup	dry white wine	125 mL
¼ cup	chopped fresh parsley or cilantro	60 mL
2 tbsp	drained rinsed capers	30 mL
1 lb	skinless salmon or trout fillets, cut into chunks	500 g
24	jumbo shrimp, shelled and deveined	24
24	mussels or scallops, cleaned	24

1. In the bottom of a flameproof tagine, heat oil over medium heat. Add garlic and Berbere and cook, stirring, for 3 to 4 minutes or until garlic is softened but not colored. Add carrots, parsnips, zucchini, onion, and red and green bell peppers and cook, stirring, for 1 minute to coat with oil and spices.

2. Add stock, wine, parsley and capers and bring to a boil. Stir in salmon, shrimp and mussels. Cover with tagine lid, reduce heat to low and simmer gently, stirring once or twice, for 15 to 20 minutes or until fish is opaque and flakes easily with a fork, shrimp is bright pink and opaque and shells of mussels are open (discard any that remain shut).

Lobster and Shrimp with Fennel and Spinach

Makes 4 to 6 servings

If you cook the rice separately, it will take far less time than in the tagine, but this is such a convenient way to prepare a meal, I add the rice and simply do something else while the vegetables and rice cook. The lobster makes this a meal fit for guests and it is available frozen in tins so I always have it on hand for family meals as well.

Tip

Where I live, lobster meat is available in 2 lb (1 kg) tins in the freezer section where shrimp and other frozen fish are kept. This form is convenient and it offers the perfect solution for people who have no access to fresh lobster. Always thaw seafood in the refrigerator — a 2-lb (1 kg) tin will take 6 to 8 hours to thaw in the refrigerator.

● **Medium or large tagine**

2 tbsp	avocado or olive oil	30 mL
1 tbsp	butter	15 mL
2	onions, cut in half and sliced	2
½	fennel bulb, chopped	½
6	cloves garlic, sliced	6
1 tsp	Harissa (page 45) or hot pepper flakes	5 mL
1 tsp	ground coriander	5 mL
½ tsp	ground cinnamon	2 mL
¾ cup	short-grain brown rice	175 mL
1¼ cups	chicken broth	300 mL
¼ cup	heavy or whipping (35%) cream	60 mL
18	jumbo shrimp, shelled and deveined	18
2 cups	baby spinach	500 mL
11 oz	lobster meat (thawed if frozen) (see Tip, left)	320 g
4	sprigs fresh flat-leaf parsley	4

1. In bottom of flameproof tagine, heat oil and melt butter over medium heat. Add onions, fennel and garlic and cook, stirring, for 5 minutes. Add harissa, coriander, cinnamon and rice and cook, stirring constantly, for 2 minutes. Add broth and bring to a boil. Cover with tagine lid, reduce heat to low and cook, stirring once, for 1 hour.

2. Test rice for tenderness and liquid. If rice is still chewy with an excess of liquid, remove tagine lid and gently simmer over medium heat until tender and most of the liquid is absorbed, about 30 minutes.

3. Stir cream and shrimp into rice and vegetables in tagine. Cook and stir over low to medium-low heat for 3 to 4 minutes or until sauce is bubbly and shrimp has turned bright pink and opaque. Add spinach and lobster and gently simmer for about 1 minute until spinach is wilted and lobster is heated through. Garnish with parsley just before serving.

Minted Lemon Whitefish

Makes 4 servings

In this fresh-tasting dish, white fish is marinated in a herb and spice blend and gently simmered in a lemon and mint-spiked sauce. New potatoes and fresh spring peas lend a seasonal presence to this dish.

Tips

Sometimes it is difficult to purchase fish to the exact weight, therefore I have given a range. The important thing to remember when purchasing ingredients for tagine cooking is to know the capacity of your own tagine.

The Moroccans tend to use spearmint a lot in dips, drinks, couscous and tagine dishes. I actually prefer the taste of peppermint over that of spearmint, so that is what I use, and either variety will work in this recipe.

● **Medium tagine**

¼ cup	Taklia Spice Blend (page 52) or Chermoula Moroccan Rub (page 40)	60 mL
1½ cups	chicken broth or fish stock, divided	375 mL
1 to 1½ lbs	skinless white fish fillets, such as cod, black sea bass or Pacific halibut (see Tips, left)	500 to 750 g
2 tbsp	avocado or olive oil	30 mL
1	onion, cut into eighths	1
1	Preserved Lemon or Frozen Lemon (pages 48 and 49), finely chopped	1
24	small new potatoes	24
2 cups	shelled fresh peas	500 mL
1 tbsp	fresh chopped spearmint or peppermint (see Tips, left)	15 mL

1. In a shallow dish, combine spice blend and ½ cup (125 mL) of the broth. Cut fish into 1½-inch (4 cm) chunks and toss in spiced paste mixture. Cover and let stand for 30 minutes.

2. In the bottom of a flameproof tagine, heat oil over medium heat. Add onion and cook, stirring, for 5 minutes. Add remaining 1 cup (250 mL) of broth, flesh with juice of lemon and potatoes. Bring to a boil. Cover with tagine lid, reduce heat to low and simmer for 20 to 30 minutes or until potatoes show slight resistance when pierced with the tip of a knife.

3. Stir in fish with marinade and add peas. Replace cover and simmer gently for 15 to 20 minutes or until fish is opaque and flakes easily with a fork. Garnish with mint.

Pacific Halibut, Fennel and Black Olives

**Makes
4 servings**

The rich and flavorful sauce in this fish tagine makes a fine soup and, if served with thick slices of crusty bread, it can be mopped up easily.

Variation

Instead of halibut, use any firm whitefish such as haddock, black sea bass, catfish or cod.

● **Medium tagine**

2 tbsp	avocado or olive oil	30 mL
1	onion, cut into eighths	1
3	cloves garlic, sliced	3
1 tbsp	Berbere (page 42) or store-bought garam masala	15 mL
½	fennel bulb, thinly sliced	½
½	red bell pepper, sliced into strips	½
24	small new potatoes	24
1½ cups	chicken broth or fish stock	375 mL
	Juice of ½ fresh lemon or Frozen Lemon (page 49)	
1 lb	fresh green or yellow beans, trimmed	500 g
1 to 1½ lbs	Pacific halibut, skin on one side (see Tip, page 123)	500 to 750 g

1. In the bottom of a flameproof tagine, heat oil over medium heat. Add onion, garlic and Berbere and cook, stirring, for 5 minutes. Add fennel, bell pepper and potatoes and cook, stirring, for 1 minute to coat the vegetables with seasoning. Add broth and lemon juice and bring to a boil. Cover with tagine lid, reduce heat to low and simmer for 15 to 20 minutes or until potatoes show slight resistance when pierced with the tip of a knife.

2. Add beans to the vegetables and lay fish fillets over vegetables, skin side down. Replace cover and simmer gently for 15 to 20 minutes or until fish is opaque and flakes easily with a fork.

Poached Salmon with Caper Sauce

**Makes
4 servings**

In the summer I serve this cold with a noodle or rice salad or simply over salad greens. If you use a large tagine, the salmon does not need to be cut, and keeping it whole makes a beautiful presentation on a platter.

● **Large tagine**

Poached salmon

1¼ cups	chicken broth	300 mL
1	salmon fillet or piece (about 1¼ lbs/625 g)	1
2	stalks celery, chopped	2
1	onion, quartered	1
¼ cup	dry white wine	60 mL
2 tbsp	freshly squeezed lemon juice	30 mL

Caper Sauce

2 tsp	cornstarch	10 mL
1 tsp	granulated sugar	5 mL
2 tbsp	water	30 mL
1 tbsp	chopped capers	15 mL
2 tsp	Dijon mustard	10 mL
½ cup	Drained Yogurt (page 117)	125 mL

1. *Poached Salmon:* In the bottom of a flameproof tagine, bring chicken broth to a boil over medium heat. Add salmon, celery, onion, wine and lemon juice. Cover with tagine lid, reduce heat to low and simmer gently, for 10 to 15 minutes or until fish flakes easily with a fork. Transfer fish to a heated platter and keep warm. If you plan to serve it cold, lift salmon out of poaching liquid onto a platter. Let cool, cover tightly and refrigerate for 1 hour or overnight.

2. Increase heat to medium and boil poaching liquid for 10 minutes or until reduced to about 1 cup (250 mL).

3. *Caper Sauce:* Meanwhile, in a small bowl, combine cornstarch and sugar. Stir in water to form a smooth paste. Add to reduced poaching liquid and cook, stirring constantly, for 2 to 3 minutes or until sauce is thickened. Remove from heat and stir in capers, mustard and yogurt. Pass sauce separately or drizzle over fish on the platter. Sauce may be kept, covered, in the refrigerator until ready to use.

Saffron Shrimp with Avocado

Use avocado oil if possible in this tagine because it will add depth of flavor to the sauce. Serve the tagine over long-grain or Basmati rice because this golden sauce is filled with the sunlit essence of the Mediterranean coast.

Tip

I recommend the use of organic, cold-pressed extra virgin avocado oil in the tagine recipes in this book because it is excellent for medium to high heat cooking. Unlike other polyunsaturated oils, olive oil in particular, avocado oil does not break down under high heat cooking. It is an excellent source of vitamin E and contains beneficial omega-3, 6 and 9 fatty acids.

● **Medium tagine**

20	saffron threads	20
¾ cup	chicken broth, divided	175 mL
2 tbsp	avocado or olive oil	30 mL
1 tbsp	butter	15 mL
1	onion, chopped	1
½	fennel bulb, chopped	½
4	cloves garlic, minced	4
1 tbsp	ground turmeric	15 mL
24	jumbo shrimp, shelled and deveined	24
2 tbsp	freshly squeezed lemon juice	30 mL
2	avocados, sliced	2
2 tbsp	chopped fresh flat-leaf parsley	30 mL

1. In a bowl, combine saffron and ¼ cup (60 mL) of the broth. Set aside.

2. In the bottom of a flameproof tagine, heat oil and melt butter over medium heat. Add onion, fennel and garlic and cook, stirring, for 5 minutes. Stir in turmeric until incorporated. Add remaining broth and bring to a boil. Stir in saffron with broth and shrimp. Cover with tagine lid, reduce heat to low and simmer, stirring once, for 5 to 7 minutes or until shrimp have turned bright pink and opaque.

3. Add lemon juice, avocados and parsley and cook, stirring constantly, until avocados are heated through.

Salmon with Mushrooms and Capers

Makes 4 servings

The fish gently steams on top of the vegetables in this quick, easy and healthy dish. You can use almost any vegetable and most medium to firm fish remains intact, especially if the skin is attached to one side of the fillet. It's a one-pot convenience meal, on the table in less than 45 minutes.

Tip

Once the fish is cooked, remove skin using a paring knife. It will slip easily away from the flesh.

● **Medium tagine**

4 tbsp	avocado or olive oil, divided	60 mL
1	onion, cut in half and sliced	1
2 cups	sliced cauliflower florets	500 mL
2	portobello mushrooms, cut in half and sliced	2
1 tbsp	Ras el Hanout (page 50) or store-bought	15 mL
¼ cup	drained rinsed capers	60 mL
1 lb	salmon, cod or haddock pieces, skin on one side	500 g

1. In the bottom of a flameproof tagine, heat 2 tbsp (30 mL) of the oil over medium heat. Add onion and cauliflower, cover with tagine lid and cook, stirring occasionally, for 10 minutes. Add remaining oil, mushrooms, ras el hanout and capers. Replace cover, reduce heat to medium-low and cook, stirring occasionally, for 5 minutes or until onions are soft and lightly browned.

2. Meanwhile, cut fish into 4 equal pieces if still in one piece. Lay fish on top of the vegetables, skin side up. Cover, reduce heat to low and simmer gently for 15 to 20 minutes or until fish is opaque and flakes easily with a fork.

Tuna Steaks in Spiced Tomato Sauce

Makes 4 servings

Tuna is a dry and firm-textured fish that is perfect for moist tagine cooking. When grilling tuna, I use a high heat and cook the steaks only for about 4 minutes, turning once, which results in the fish being rare. In this dish, the hot and spicy Harissa seasoning is added to tomatoes for a nippy effect and I cook the fish to a medium-rare state. You can substitute any of the Moroccan spice blends (starting on page 38) or alter the amount of Harissa to suit your taste and cook the tuna to the degree of doneness you prefer.

Tip

If you use another firm-fleshed fish, such as Pacific halibut, haddock, snapper or black sea bass, the mark of doneness is when the fish turns opaque and flakes easily with a fork.

● **Medium tagine**

2 tbsp	avocado or olive oil	30 mL
1	onion, cut in half and sliced	1
1	can (19 oz/540 mL) diced tomatoes with juice	1
¼ cup	chopped fresh flat-leaf parsley or cilantro	60 mL
2 tbsp	drained rinsed capers	30 mL
2 to 4 tsp	Harissa (page 45) or hot pepper flakes	10 to 20 mL
1½ to 2 lbs	tuna steaks (see Tip, left, and page 123)	750 to 1 kg

1. In the bottom of a flameproof tagine, heat oil over medium heat. Add onion and cook, stirring, for 5 minutes. Add tomatoes with juice, parsley, capers and Harissa to taste and bring to a boil. Lay fish in the sauce, sliding steaks around and moving vegetables away from bottom so that flesh is in direct contact with bottom of tagine. Cover with tagine lid, reduce heat to low and simmer gently for 5 minutes. Using tongs, turn fish over, replace lid and cook for 3 to 5 minutes or until fish is opaque on both sides and is light pink on the inside. Cook longer if desired.

Vegetables

Algerian Chickpea and Cauliflower Tagine

**Makes
4 servings**

Chickpeas have a firm and grainy texture that stands up to tagine cooking, but you can substitute lentils or other beans in this dish.

Tip

I recommend the use of organic, cold-pressed extra virgin avocado oil in the tagine recipes in this book because it is excellent for medium to high heat cooking. Unlike other polyunsaturated oils, olive oil in particular, avocado oil does not break down under high heat cooking. It is an excellent source of vitamin E and contains beneficial omega-3, 6 and 9 fatty acids.

● **Medium tagine**

3 tbsp	avocado or olive oil	45 mL
1	onion, cut into quarters	1
4	cloves garlic, sliced	4
1 tbsp	Bahrat Spice Blend (page 39) or store-bought garam masala	15 mL
2	red bell peppers, chopped	2
2 cups	sliced cauliflower florets	500 mL
1	can (14 oz/398 mL) diced tomatoes with juices	1
1	can (14 to 19 oz/398 to 540 mL) chickpeas, drained and rinsed	1
2 tbsp	drained rinsed capers, optional	30 mL

1. In the bottom of a flameproof tagine, heat oil over medium heat. Add onion, garlic and spice blend and cook, stirring, for 5 minutes. Stir in bell peppers and cauliflower. Cover with tagine lid, reduce heat to low and simmer for 12 to 15 minutes or until vegetables are tender.

2. Add tomatoes with juice and chickpeas and bring to a boil over medium heat. Stir in capers, if using, and heat through.

Baked Eggs with Mediterranean Vegetables

**Makes
4 servings**

Eggs are easy to make
in the tagine and are a
good source of protein
for vegetarian meals. This
dish is colorful, fresh and
very easy to make. It's
another workday lunch
or quick dinner. I always
use farm fresh large
brown eggs in this dish.

Tips

Serve with warmed pita
triangles, bagels or flatbread.

To increase the servings, use
a medium to large tagine, add
another tomato and pepper
and a couple more eggs.

● **Medium tagine**

3 tbsp	avocado or olive oil	45 mL
1	onion, coarsely chopped	1
2	cloves garlic, chopped	2
1 tbsp	Bahrat Spice Blend (page 39) or store-bought garam masala	15 mL
3	red or yellow bell peppers, cut into thin strips	3
2 cups	sliced mushrooms	500 mL
20	cherry tomatoes, cut in half	20
5	green olives, thinly sliced	5
4	large eggs	4

1. In the bottom of a flameproof tagine, heat oil over medium heat. Add onion, garlic and spice blend and cook, stirring, for 5 minutes. Stir in bell peppers, mushrooms, tomatoes and olives. Cover with tagine lid, reduce heat to low and simmer for 12 to 15 minutes or until vegetables are tender.

2. Using a wooden spoon, move the vegetables around to make round pocket spaces for eggs. Crack eggs into pockets, cover with tagine lid and simmer for 4 to 5 minutes or until whites have turned opaque and yolks are glossy and thick.

Broad Beans with Tomatoes and Olives

Makes 4 servings

With both Moroccan spices and Za'atar, this tagine is full bodied and delicious.

Tip

Native to North Africa, broad beans (*Vicia faba*), also known as fava beans, are large and mealy-textured, although softer than chickpeas. In North Africa and the Mediterranean, they are usually eaten fresh in the summer when young and tender. If you have access to fresh beans, use 2 cups (500 mL) in place of the canned and add with the potatoes.

● **Medium tagine**

3 tbsp	avocado or olive oil	45 mL
1	onion, coarsely chopped	1
1 tbsp	Moroccan Cinnamon Spice Blend (page 47) or store-bought garam masala	15 mL
1 tsp	Za'atar (page 54) or dried oregano	5 mL
¼ cup	tomato juice or water	60 mL
1 lb	small new potatoes	500 g
20	cherry tomatoes	20
10	green olives, cut in half	10
1	can (14 to 19 oz/398 to 540 mL) broad beans or white kidney beans, drained and rinsed (see Tip, left)	1

1. In the bottom of a flameproof tagine, heat oil over medium heat. Add onion, spice blend and za'atar and cook, stirring, for 5 minutes. Add tomato juice and bring to a boil. Stir in potatoes and tomatoes. Cover with tagine lid, reduce heat to low and simmer, stirring occasionally, for 12 to 15 minutes or until potatoes are tender. Stir in olives and broad beans, cover and simmer for 3 to 5 minutes or until heated through.

Carrots and Pumpkin with Apricots and Almonds

Makes 4 servings

Caramelized shallots and honeyed vegetables would make this a too-sweet dish without the tartness of the lemon. You can adjust the honey to suit your taste.

● **Medium tagine**

3 tbsp	avocado or olive oil	45 mL
6	shallots, cut in half	6
1 tbsp	Bahrat Spice Blend (page 39) or store-bought garam masala	15 mL
⅔ cup	water or freshly squeezed orange juice	150 mL
	Juice of 1 lemon	
2 tbsp	liquid honey or to taste	30 mL
2 cups	diced pumpkin or squash	500 mL
2 cups	diced carrots	500 mL

1. In the bottom of a flameproof tagine, heat oil over medium heat. Add shallots and spice blend and cook, stirring, for 5 minutes. Add water, lemon juice and honey and bring to a boil. Stir in pumpkin and carrots. Cover with tagine lid, reduce heat to low and simmer, stirring occasionally, for 30 to 45 minutes or until vegetables are tender.

Chickpea and Broad Bean Tagine

Makes 4 servings

I have found that there are a few canned vegetables that are almost as good as fresh, and they are tomatoes and legumes. Find an organic brand and stock them in your pantry for everyday meals.

Tip

If you have access to fresh beans, use 2 cups (500 mL) in place of the canned.

● **Medium tagine**

3 tbsp	avocado or olive oil	45 mL
1	onion, coarsely chopped	1
1	carrot, chopped	1
1 tbsp	Berbere (page 42) or store-bought garam masala	15 mL
1	can (19 oz/540 mL) diced tomatoes with juice	1
1	can (14 to 19 oz/398 to 540 mL) chickpeas, drained and rinsed	1
1	can (14 to 19 oz/398 to 540 mL) broad beans or white kidney beans, drained and rinsed (see Tip, left)	1

1. In the bottom of a flameproof tagine, heat oil over medium heat. Add onion, carrot and Berbere and cook, stirring, for 5 minutes. Add tomatoes with juice and bring to a boil. Stir in chickpeas and broad beans. Cover with tagine lid, reduce heat to low and simmer, stirring occasionally, for 15 to 20 minutes or until carrots are tender. To thicken the stew, mash some of the chickpeas and broad beans and stir into the sauce.

Coconut Eggplant and Chickpea Tagine

Makes 4 servings

Dates soften into the coconut milk, making a slightly sweet sauce for the zucchini and eggplant. Use baby eggplants when you can find them.

● **Medium tagine**

3 tbsp	avocado or olive oil	45 mL
2	onions, cut into eighths	2
2	baby eggplants (about 12 oz/ 375 g total), diced	2
1 tbsp	Berbere (page 42) or store-bought garam masala	15 mL
1	medium zucchini, diced	1
2 tsp	ground turmeric	10 mL
1 tsp	cayenne pepper, optional	5 mL
1 cup	coconut milk	250 mL
1	can (14 to 19 oz/398 to 540 mL) chickpeas, drained and rinsed	1

1. In the bottom of a flameproof tagine, heat oil over medium heat. Add onions, eggplants and Berbere and cook, stirring, for 5 minutes. Add zucchini, turmeric, cayenne pepper, if using, and coconut milk. Cover with tagine lid, reduce heat to low and simmer for 15 minutes or until vegetables are tender. Add chickpeas and heat through over medium heat. To thicken the stew, mash some of the chickpeas and stir into the sauce.

Eggplant and Lentil Tagine

Makes 4 servings

I like the baby eggplants because they are usually more sweet and tender, with skin that is thinner than the larger varieties, although any of the several types of eggplant will work in this dish.

● **Medium tagine**

2 tbsp	avocado or olive oil	30 mL
1 tbsp	butter	15 mL
2	onions, cut into quarters	2
1 tbsp	Berbere (page 42) or store-bought garam masala	15 mL
3	baby eggplants or 1 large eggplant (about 1½ lbs/750 g), cut into lengthwise wedges	3
4	cloves garlic, chopped	4
¼ cup	chicken broth or water	60 mL
1	can (14 to 19 oz/398 to 540 mL) lentils, drained and rinsed	1
½ cup	chopped raisins or dates	125 mL

1. In the bottom of a flameproof tagine, heat oil and melt butter over medium heat. Add onions and Berbere and cook, stirring, for 10 minutes or until soft and light golden. Add eggplants and garlic, reduce heat and cook, stirring frequently, for 7 minutes or until eggplant is soft and lightly browned. Add broth, lentils and raisins. Cover with tagine lid, reduce heat to low and simmer, stirring occasionally, for 7 to 12 minutes or until lentils are heated through.

Fall Vegetable Tagine

Although tagine dishes are convenient and may use any seasonal vegetable, harvest time is the perfect time to make these tasty stews.

Variation

Turnip and cauliflower can be replaced with any fall vegetables such as cabbage, kale or eggplant or any variety of squash or pumpkin.

● **Medium tagine**

3 tbsp	avocado or olive oil	45 mL
2	onions, cut into quarters	2
4	cloves garlic, coarsely chopped	4
1	red bell pepper, chopped	1
1 tbsp	Ras el Hanout (page 50) or store-bought	15 mL
1½ cups	Green Tomato and Apple Jam (page 152) or tomato sauce	375 mL
½ cup	water	125 mL
2 cups	diced turnip	500 mL
2 cups	sliced cauliflower florets	500 mL
1	can (14 to 19 oz/398 to 540 mL) chickpeas, drained and rinsed	1
½ cup	sunflower seeds	125 mL

1. In the bottom of a flameproof tagine, heat oil over medium heat. Add onions, garlic, bell pepper and ras el hanout and cook, stirring, for 5 minutes. Add jam, water, turnip, cauliflower and chickpeas. Cover with tagine lid, reduce heat to low and simmer for 45 minutes or until vegetables are tender. Garnish with sunflower seeds.

Fava Bean and Potato Tagine

Makes 4 to 6 servings

This stew is best if made in the spring when the potatoes are new and artichokes and fennel bulbs are in season. Fava beans, also known as broad beans, are shucked and added to the stew at the very last moment because it only takes a few minutes for them to cook.

Tip

Use canned fava beans if fresh are not available.

● **Medium or large tagine**

2	fresh lemons	2
6	medium artichokes	6
3 tbsp	avocado or olive oil	45 mL
2	onions, cut into quarters	2
3	cloves garlic, coarsely chopped	3
1 tbsp	Berbere (page 42) or store-bought garam masala	15 mL
12	small new potatoes, cut in half	12
1	fennel bulb, chopped	1
3	carrots, chopped	3
½ cup	water or chicken broth	125 mL
1 lb	fresh fava beans or peas (see Tip, left)	500 g
¼ cup	chopped fresh parsley	60 mL

1. Zest ½ lemon and set aside. Juice lemons and pour into a large bowl and set aside. Working with one artichoke at a time, snap off the dark-green outer leaves, leaving the pale, tender inner leaves on the stem. Trim off all but 1-inch (2.5 cm) of the stem. Trim away the top third of the artichoke leaves. Use a paring knife to peel away the tough outer layer of the stem and to remove the base of the leaves. Cut the artichoke in half and half again. Trim away and discard the hairy choke and any thorny inner leaves of each quarter. As the artichokes are cut and trimmed, toss the quarters into the bowl with the lemon juice.

2. In the bottom of a flameproof tagine, heat oil over medium heat. Add onions, garlic and Berbere and cook, stirring, for 5 minutes. Add potatoes, fennel and carrots. Stir in water and bring to a boil. Cover with tagine lid, reduce heat to low and simmer for 35 minutes or until vegetables are tender.

3. Add fava beans, reserved lemon zest and parsley and simmer for 2 to 3 minutes or until beans are tender.

Fennel, Artichoke and Potato Tagine

**Makes
4 servings**

The anise of the fennel bulb is mild and adds a hint of licorice to the delicately seasoned vegetables in this dish. The feta cheese adds the typical tangy note while boosting the protein.

Tips

I use either sweet or russet (Idaho) potatoes, but the sweet potatoes are more in keeping with traditional tagine flavors.

To toast seeds in a tagine: In the bottom of a tagine, toast sesame seeds over medium-low heat, stirring frequently, for 1 to 2 minutes or just until seeds color slightly. Remove from tagine to cool or they will continue to cook, especially if the base is cast iron.

● **Medium tagine**

3 tbsp	avocado or olive oil	45 mL
2	red onions, each cut into eighths	2
2	cloves garlic, coarsely chopped	2
1	slice candied ginger, finely chopped	1
1 tbsp	La Kama Spice Blend (page 44) or Berbere (page 42)	15 mL
1	large sweet potato, cut into lengthwise wedges (about 1½ lbs/750 g) (see Tips, left)	1
2 cups	diced fennel bulb	500 mL
1	can (14 oz/398 mL) artichoke hearts, drained and cut in half	1
1 cup	crumbled or finely diced feta cheese	250 mL
½ cup	toasted or plain sesame seeds (see Tips, left)	125 mL

1. In the bottom of a flameproof tagine, heat oil over medium heat. Add red onions, garlic, ginger and spice blend and cook, stirring, for 5 minutes. Add sweet potato, fennel and artichokes. Cover with tagine lid, reduce heat to low and simmer, stirring occasionally, for 15 to 20 minutes or until vegetables are tender. Toss vegetables with feta cheese. Garnish with sesame seeds.

Honey-Ginger Vegetable Tagine

Makes 4 servings

Lightly sweetened with honey and warmed with two types of ginger, this tagine is perfect for serving on a long winter evening. Most of the ingredients should be in the pantry, making this a quick weeknight meal.

● **Medium tagine**

3 tbsp	avocado or olive oil	45 mL
2	onions, cut into quarters	2
2	cloves garlic, coarsely chopped	2
1	slice candied ginger, finely chopped	1
1 tbsp	La Kama Spice Blend (page 44) or Berbere (page 42)	15 mL
¾ cup	chicken broth or water	175 mL
2 tbsp	liquid honey	30 mL
1 tbsp	grated fresh gingerroot	15 mL
3	potatoes, cut lengthwise into wedges (about 1½ lbs/750 g total)	3
2 cups	sliced cauliflower florets	500 mL
1 cup	fresh or frozen peas	250 mL
½ cup	toasted or plain sesame seeds	125 mL

1. In the bottom of a flameproof tagine, heat oil over medium heat. Add onions, garlic, candied ginger and spice blend and cook, stirring, for 5 minutes. Add broth, honey and ginger and bring to a boil. Stir in potatoes, cauliflower and peas. Cover with tagine lid, reduce heat to low and simmer, stirring occasionally, for 12 to 15 minutes or until vegetables are tender. Garnish with sesame seeds.

Lentil and Almond Tagine

Makes 4 servings

Lentils add protein to this substantial and filling vegetable tagine. The nuts are toasted for extra crispness and flavor.

Tips

Use pumpkin, yam, sweet potato, butternut squash or acorn squash in this vegetarian tagine.

To dry roast nuts in a tagine: In the bottom of a tagine, toast almonds over medium-low heat, stirring frequently, for 2 to 3 minutes or just until nuts color slightly. Remove from tagine to cool or they will continue to cook, especially if the base is cast iron.

● **Medium or large tagine**

2 tbsp	avocado or olive oil	30 mL
2	onions, coarsely chopped	2
1	fresh hot chile pepper, chopped	1
½	red bell pepper, chopped	½
1 tbsp	sweet paprika	15 mL
2 tsp	Bahrat Spice Blend (page 39) or Ras el Hanout (page 50)	10 mL
1 cup	yellow, red or brown lentils, rinsed	250 mL
1	can (19 oz/540 mL) diced tomatoes with juice	1
2 cups	diced pumpkin or squash (see Tips, left)	500 mL
¼ cup	ground almonds	60 mL
2 cups	shredded Swiss chard	500 mL
½ cup	toasted whole almonds (see Tips, left)	125 mL

1. In the bottom of a flameproof tagine, heat oil over medium heat. Add onions, chile pepper, bell pepper, paprika and spice blend and cook, stirring, for 5 minutes. Add lentils and cook, stirring, for 2 minutes. Add tomatoes with juice and bring to a boil.

2. Cover with tagine lid, reduce heat to low and simmer, for 20 minutes or until lentils are tender. Add pumpkin and ground almonds, replace lid and simmer for 15 minutes. Stir in Swiss chard, replace lid and simmer for 5 minutes or until greens are wilted and pumpkin is tender. Garnish with whole almonds.

Moroccan Vegetable Tagine

**Makes
4 servings**

Sweetened with honey,
thickened with tahini
and delicately spiced,
this North African stew
resembles the French
ratatouille.

● **Medium or large tagine**

2 tbsp	avocado or olive oil	30 mL
1	onion, cut in half and sliced	1
1	fresh hot chile pepper, chopped	1
1	red bell pepper, chopped	1
1 tbsp	sweet paprika	15 mL
2 tsp	Bahrat Spice Blend (page 39) or Ras el Hanout (page 50)	10 mL
2 cups	chopped eggplant	500 mL
1	zucchini, chopped	1
1	can (19 oz/540 mL) diced tomatoes with juice	1
2 tbsp	liquid honey	30 mL
2 tbsp	tahini	30 mL
1 cup	packed baby spinach leaves	250 mL
¼ cup	sesame seeds	60 mL

1. In the bottom of a flameproof tagine, heat oil over medium heat. Add onion, chile pepper, bell pepper, paprika and spice blend and cook, stirring, for 5 minutes. Add eggplant and zucchini and cook, stirring, for 2 minutes. Add tomatoes with juices and honey and bring to a boil.

2. Cover with tagine lid, reduce heat to low and simmer for 15 to 20 minutes or until vegetables are tender. Add tahini and stir until incorporated. Stir in spinach, replace lid and simmer for 5 minutes or until wilted. Garnish with sesame seeds.

Onion and Leek Tagine

Makes 4 servings

With the caramelized onions and leeks, this tagine does not need any extra sweetening. Fresh apricots or peaches add to the complex taste.

Tip

Leeks tend to gather soil between the leaves as they push upward through the garden. **To clean leeks:** Split leeks in half and hold under cool running water, separating the leaves to let the water reach between the leaves and remove grit and soil.

● **Medium tagine**

3 tbsp	avocado or olive oil	45 mL
1 tbsp	butter	15 mL
2	onions, coarsely chopped	2
1	leek, white and tender green parts, split and chopped (see Tip, left)	1
3	cloves garlic, coarsely chopped	3
1 tbsp	La Kama Spice Blend (page 44) or store-bought garam masala	15 mL
2 cups	diced potato	500 mL
1 cup	diced turnip or rutabaga	250 mL
4	fresh apricots or peaches, sliced	4
½ cup	chicken broth or water	125 mL

1. In the bottom of a flameproof tagine, heat oil and melt butter over medium heat. Add onions and leek and cook, stirring, for 10 to 12 minutes or until soft and light golden. Add garlic and spice blend and cook, stirring, for 3 to 5 minutes or until garlic is soft. Stir in potato, turnip and apricots. Add broth and bring to a boil. Cover with tagine lid, reduce heat to low and simmer, stirring occasionally, for 35 to 40 minutes or until vegetables are tender.

Mushroom Tagine with Eggplant and Squash

Makes 4 servings

With two kinds of mushrooms and creamy eggplant, this tagine is the perfect one-dish meal for serving over red or brown or mahogany rice. The white kidney beans are smooth in texture in the sauce, but you could use black-eyed peas or chickpeas.

● **Medium tagine**

3 tbsp	avocado or olive oil	45 mL
1	onion, coarsely chopped	1
6	cloves garlic, thickly sliced	6
1 tbsp	Ras el Hanout (page 50) or store-bought	15 mL
2 tbsp	butter	30 mL
12	cremini mushrooms, coarsely chopped	12
1	eggplant (about 1 lb/500 g), peeled and diced	1
1 cup	diced squash or pumpkin	250 mL
1	cayenne pepper, crumbled, optional	1
18	cherry tomatoes, cut in half	18
1	can (14 to 19 oz/398 to 540 mL) white kidney beans, drained and rinsed	1
1 cup	chopped kale, Swiss chard, cabbage or bok choy	250 mL
2	portobello mushrooms, stems trimmed	2
¼ cup	crumbled feta cheese	60 mL
	Cooked rice or couscous	

1. In the bottom of a flameproof tagine, heat oil over medium heat. Add onion, garlic and ras el hanout and cook, stirring frequently, for 5 minutes. Add butter, cremini mushrooms, eggplant and squash and cook, stirring frequently, for 5 minutes.

2. Stir in cayenne, if using. Add tomatoes and kidney beans. Cover with tagine lid, reduce heat to low and simmer for 15 minutes or until vegetables are tender.

I recommend the use of organic, cold-pressed extra virgin avocado oil in the tagine recipes in this book because it is excellent for medium to high heat cooking. Unlike other polyunsaturated oils, olive oil in particular, avocado oil does not break down under high heat cooking. It is an excellent source of vitamin E and contains beneficial omega-3, 6 and 9 fatty acids.

3. Stir kale into tagine. Nestle portobello mushrooms, gill sides up, into vegetables but do not let vegetables cover the tops. Sprinkle feta cheese over mushroom caps. Replace cover and simmer for 15 to 20 minutes or until portobello mushrooms are tender and cheese is melted.

4. To serve, remove and cut portobello mushrooms in half. Spoon mushroom tagine over cooked rice or couscous and top each serving with half a portobello mushroom.

Sweet Potato and Turnip Tagine

**Makes
4 servings**

I like to make this tagine with very little liquid, but you can add more at any point in the cooking process if you prefer to have a dish with more sauce.

● **Medium tagine**

2 tbsp	avocado or olive oil	30 mL
2 tbsp	butter	30 mL
2	onions, coarsely chopped	2
3	cloves garlic, coarsely chopped	3
1 tbsp	Ras el Hanout (page 50) or store-bought	15 mL
2 cups	diced sweet potato	500 mL
1 cup	diced turnip or squash	250 mL
½ cup	freshly squeezed orange juice or water (approx.)	125 mL
1	can (14 to 19 oz/398 to 540 mL) chickpeas, drained and rinsed	1
1 cup	dried apricot slivers	250 mL

1. In the bottom of a flameproof tagine, heat oil and melt butter over medium heat. Add onions, garlic and ras el hanout and cook, stirring, for 5 minutes. Add sweet potato, turnip and orange juice and bring to a boil. Cover with tagine lid, reduce heat to low and simmer, stirring occasionally and adding more orange juice if required, for 45 minutes.

2. Stir in chickpeas and apricots. Replace cover and simmer, for 10 to 15 minutes or until vegetables are tender and apricots are plump.

Dips, Souk Food and Sauces

Dips

Souk Food

continued...

Sauces

Aïoli

Makes 1¼ cups (300 mL)

Aïoli is a traditional Mediterranean egg mayonnaise meant to be served with vegetables. The garlic is the correct amount but you can use less to suit your taste.

Tip

In some areas you can purchase a pasteurized liquid egg product, not to be confused with liquid egg substitutes. This is a great product for making recipes with raw eggs when you may have safety concerns. Please consult your medical professional prior to making or serving dishes with raw eggs if this is a concern for you.

● **Food processor or blender**

1 cup	avocado or olive oil	250 mL
6	cloves garlic, crushed	6
3	eggs, at room temperature (see Tip, left)	3
1 tbsp	freshly squeezed lemon juice	15 mL
¼ tsp	salt	1 mL

1. In a small saucepan, gently heat oil with garlic over low heat for about 15 minutes. Do not let oil smoke. Let cool to room temperature.

2. In a sieve over a small bowl, strain oil, pressing with back of a spoon to extract soft solids from garlic. Discard remaining garlic.

3. In a food processor or blender, process eggs, lemon juice and salt for about 10 seconds or until blended. With the motor running, add oil, a few drops at a time, through opening in feed tube, then in a thin steady stream until all oil is absorbed and mixture is thickened. Scrape into a small bowl. Serve immediately or refrigerate until ready to serve. Store, tightly covered, in the refrigerator for up to 2 days.

Chunky Fig and Date Aïoli

Makes 1½ cups (375 mL)

With the addition of figs and dates, the resulting mayonnaise is sweeter and darker in color. Use it with fish or chicken or drizzle over fresh fruit.

Tip

I recommend the use of organic, cold-pressed extra virgin macadamia oil because it is high in monounsaturated fats and its buttery taste is exceptional in aïoli. Use it wherever avocado or olive oil is called for in these recipes.

● **Food processor or blender**

3	eggs, at room temperature (see Tip, page 149)	3
1 tbsp	freshly squeezed lemon juice	15 mL
¼ tsp	salt	1 mL
2 tbsp	finely chopped dates	30 mL
1 tbsp	finely chopped figs	15 mL
1 cup	macadamia or olive oil (see Tip, left)	250 mL

1. In a food processor or blender, process eggs, lemon juice and salt for about 10 seconds or until blended. Add dates and figs and process until blended.

2. With the motor running, add oil, a few drops at a time, through opening in feed tube, then in a thin steady stream until all oil is absorbed and mixture is thickened. Scrape into a small bowl. Serve immediately or refrigerate until ready to serve. Store, tightly covered, in the refrigerator for up to 2 days.

Eggplant-Artichoke Tagine Dip

Makes 2 cups (500 mL)

This chunky mix is a quick and great-tasting spread for use with raw veggies, crackers, or served with radicchio leaves as a first course. It may be made one day in advance but tends to turn dark upon storage.

● **Small tagine**

4 tbsp	avocado or olive oil, divided	60 mL
1	onion, chopped	1
1 tbsp	Ras el Hanout (page 50) or store bought	15 mL
3 cups	diced eggplant	750 mL
3 tbsp	freshly squeezed lemon juice	45 mL
2	cloves garlic, minced	2
½ tsp	sea salt	2 mL
2 tbsp	Pomegranate Molasses (page 172) or Date Molasses (page 170)	30 mL
1	jar (6 oz/175 g) marinated artichokes, drained and coarsely chopped	1
1 cup	green olives, pitted and chopped, optional	250 mL
	Toasted pita points or radicchio leaves, optional	

1. In the bottom of a flameproof tagine, heat 2 tbsp (30 mL) oil over medium heat. Add onion and ras el hanout and cook, stirring, for 5 minutes. Stir in eggplant, lemon juice, garlic and salt. Drizzle with remaining oil. Cover with tagine lid, reduce heat to low and simmer for 12 to 15 minutes or until eggplant is soft.

2. Stir in molasses, artichokes and olives, if using, and cook, stirring occasionally, for 5 minutes. To serve, spoon onto toast points or radicchio leaves, if desired.

Green Tomato and Apple Jam

**Makes 6 cups
(1.5 L)**

A great harvest
sweet-sour sauce,
especially in those years
when the tomatoes
don't ripen as they
should. Make double
the recipe and freeze.

Tip

Freeze this jam in an airtight
container and thaw in the
refrigerator before using in
recipes. The texture will be
softer, but the taste won't
change upon freezing.

4	green tomatoes, diced and drained	4
4	apples, diced	4
1	onion, chopped	1
¼ cup	apple juice	60 mL
1 tbsp	apple cider vinegar	15 mL
1 cup	packed brown sugar	250 mL
2 tbsp	Fennel Seasoning (page 43) or Moroccan Cinnamon Spice Blend (page 47)	30 mL
	Salt and freshly ground black pepper	

1. In a large saucepan, combine tomatoes, apples, onion, apple juice and vinegar. Bring to a boil over high heat. Add brown sugar and stir until combined. Reduce heat and simmer for 25 minutes or until mixture is soft, thickened and reduced to about 6 cups (1.5 L).

2. Stir in seasoning. Simmer for 5 minutes. Add salt and pepper to taste. Let cool and store, tightly covered, in the refrigerator for up to 1 week or in the freezer for up to 3 months.

Hummus

Makes 8 to 10 servings

Keep a tin of chickpeas in the pantry and you have what it takes to boost the protein in salads and wraps. Or use this easy yet sophisticated dip with pita wedges or a mix of chopped raw vegetables. This version has less fat than the Harissa Hummus (page 154).

Tip

Tahini, an oily, beige-colored paste, is made from ground sesame seeds. It's used in hummus and other Middle Eastern dips and sauces.

● **Food processor or blender**

1	can (14 to 19 oz/398 to 540 mL) chickpeas, drained and rinsed, or 2 cups (500 mL) cooked chickpeas	1
2	cloves garlic	2
2 tbsp	tahini (see Tip, left)	30 mL
1/3 cup	avocado or olive oil	75 mL
1/3 cup	freshly squeezed lemon juice	75 mL
1/2 tsp	salt	2 mL
1/2 tsp	ground cumin	2 mL
1/4 cup	water	60 mL
1 to 2 tbsp	sesame or macadamia oil, optional	15 to 30 mL

1. In a food processor or blender, process chickpeas and garlic for about 30 seconds until finely chopped. Add tahini paste. With motor running, add avocado oil and lemon juice through opening in feed tube and process for about 15 seconds or until well mixed. Stop and scrape down the sides of the bowl. Add salt and cumin. With motor running, add water through opening in feed tube and process for about 15 seconds or until smooth.

2. Scrape purée into a serving dish. Make a few wells in the top with the back of a spoon. Drizzle sesame oil to taste, if using, over the top. Serve at room temperature. Store, tightly covered, in the refrigerator for up to 1 week.

Harissa Hummus

Makes 2½ cups (625 mL)

There are some great brands of commercial hummus on the market today and yet most of them contain chemical additives and preservatives. I still make my own hummus to use as a spread with pita as an accompaniment to any tagine. For less heat, omit the harissa.

● **Food processor or blender**

1	can (14 to 19 oz/398 to 540 mL) chickpeas, drained and rinsed, or 2 cups (500 mL) cooked chickpeas	1
4	cloves garlic	4
2 tbsp	tahini paste or peanut butter	30 mL
1 to 1½ cups	avocado or olive oil	250 to 375 mL
3 tbsp	freshly squeezed lemon juice	45 mL
1 tbsp	Harissa (page 45), or to taste	15 mL
½ tsp	salt	2 mL
½ tsp	ground cumin	2 mL

1. In a food processor or blender, process chickpeas and garlic until chopped. Add tahini paste. With motor running, add 1 cup (250 mL) of the oil slowly through opening in feed tube and process until well mixed. Stop and scrape down sides of bowl. Add more oil, 1 tbsp (15 mL) at a time, until desired consistency is achieved. Add lemon juice, harissa, salt and cumin and process until mixed into hummus. Store, tightly covered, in the refrigerator for up to 1 week.

Herbed Feta Dip

Makes 2 cups (500 mL)

Cheesy, flavorful and creamy, this dip has all the characteristics of a commercial dip and yet it is not loaded with the calories and chemicals. Use it on baked potatoes, soups and bagels or anywhere you would use sour cream.

Tip

To make Yogurt Cheese:
Set a stainless-steel strainer or colander over a bowl large enough to hold 2 cups (500 mL) of liquid. Line the strainer with a double layer of clean cheesecloth. Pour 2 cups (500 mL) of fresh plain yogurt into the lined strainer and cover the strainer with plastic wrap or fold up the edges of the cheesecloth to enclose the top of the yogurt. Set the bowl and strainer in the refrigerator and let the watery whey drain away from the yogurt solids for 8 hours or overnight. The result will be a thick, soft product that resembles cream cheese.

½	English cucumber	½
1⅓ cups	Yogurt Cheese (see Tip, left)	325 mL
1 cup	crumbled drained feta cheese	250 mL
2 cups	packed fresh spinach leaves, chopped	500 mL
¼ cup	chopped fresh chives or green onions	60 mL
2	cloves garlic, minced	2

1. Shred cucumber (peel if not organic) into a colander. Let stand in the sink or over a bowl for 30 minutes. Press or squeeze lightly to expel excess liquid.

2. In a bowl, combine cucumber, yogurt cheese, feta cheese, spinach, chives and garlic. Stir to mix well. Store, tightly covered, in the refrigerator for up to 2 days.

Roasted Garlic
and Red Pepper Pesto

Makes 2 cups (500 mL)

This pesto is bright red. Use it as a colorful garnish or to add a dash of the dramatic to salads or vegetable dishes.

● **Food processor or blender**

4	heads roasted garlic (page 157)	4
2 cups	Roasted Red Peppers (page 51), divided, or store-bought	500 mL
1 cup	fresh basil leaves	250 mL
1/4 cup	pine nuts	60 mL
1/3 cup	freshly grated Parmesan cheese	75 mL
1/2 tsp	salt	2 mL

1. Squeeze the soft flesh of each garlic clove into a food processor or blender. Add 1 cup (250 mL) of the Roasted Red Peppers, basil, pine nuts and Parmesan. Process for 30 seconds or until well blended. Add remaining Roasted Red Peppers and salt and pulse 2 or 3 times to chop peppers (being careful not to purée them).

2. Store, tightly covered, in the refrigerator for up to 1 week or in the freezer for up to 2 months.

Roasted Garlic

Makes 1 head

A handful of whole bulbs, when roasted or gently "sweated" in olive oil, morph into a sweet and meltingly tender pulpy mass with a deceptively mellow flavor. Use roasted garlic to thicken sauces.

Tips

For a larger amount of roasted garlic, you can use a small tagine to roast 3 to 6 heads of garlic on top of the stove or in the oven, following the recipe and using 6 tsp (30 mL) avocado oil for the 6 heads.

Store roasted garlic tightly covered in the refrigerator for up to 5 days. Or squeeze the cloves out of skin and place in resealable freezer bags and freeze for up to 3 months.

- **Preheat oven to 400°F (200°C)**
- **Small heatproof baking dish with lid or foil**

| 1 | whole head garlic | 1 |
| 1 tsp | olive oil | 5 mL |

1 Remove loose, papery skin from garlic head. Slice off and discard $1/4$ inch (0.5 cm) from tops of the cloves in entire head. Place garlic head, cut side up, in baking dish and drizzle with oil. Cover with a lid or foil. Bake in preheated oven for about 40 minutes or until garlic is quite soft. Transfer to a wire rack and let cool. If using a clay garlic roaster with a lid, roast at 375°F (190°C) for 35 to 40 minutes or until garlic is quite soft.

2. When garlic is cool enough to handle, squeeze cloves from their skins. They are now ready to use in any recipe that calls for roasted garlic.

Sesame Mayonnaise

Makes 1 cup (250 mL)

Homemade mayonnaise is thinner than store-bought (although it will thicken slightly upon chilling) and contains no additives.

Tip

In some areas you can purchase a pasteurized liquid egg product, not to be confused with liquid egg substitutes. This is a great product for making recipes with raw eggs when you may have safety concerns. Please consult your medical professional prior to making or serving dishes with raw eggs if this is a concern for you.

● **Food processor or blender**

1	egg, at room temperature (see Tip, left)	1
1 tbsp	rice vinegar	15 mL
1 tbsp	Dijon mustard	15 mL
1 tbsp	tamari or soy sauce	15 mL
3/4 cup	avocado or olive oil	175 mL
2 tbsp	toasted sesame oil	30 mL

1. In a food processor or blender, process egg, vinegar, mustard and tamari for about 10 seconds or until combined.

2. In a small bowl, stir together avocado oil and sesame oil. With motor running, slowly add oils through the opening in feed tube in a thin steady stream until blended and thick. Scrape into a small bowl. Serve immediately or refrigerate until ready to serve. Store, tightly covered, in the refrigerator for up to 2 days.

Tzatziki

Makes 1½ cups (375 mL)

Use this delicious spread as an all-purpose substitute for commercial mayonnaise, as a dip or spread for sandwiches, or to accompany tagine dishes, grilled fish or poultry. If you omit the garlic, the taste is refreshing and lends itself to fruit salads and dessert topping. You can add a spoonful of honey to the non-garlic version.

Tip

It is wise to peel non-organic vegetables because the peel is loaded with herbicides and washing will not eliminate them. Cucumbers are waxed in winter and they and other top-growing veggies are exposed to more chemicals than most root vegetables.

1	English cucumber (see Tip, left)	1
1⅓ cups	Yogurt Cheese (page 155)	325 mL
1	clove garlic, finely chopped	1
2 tbsp	chopped fresh mint	30 mL
2 tsp	freshly squeezed lemon juice	10 mL
	Sea salt and freshly ground black pepper	

1. Shred cucumber (peel if not organic) into a colander. Let stand in the sink or over a bowl for 30 minutes. Press or squeeze lightly to expel excess liquid.

2. In a bowl, combine cucumber, yogurt cheese, garlic, mint and lemon juice. Stir to mix well. Season to taste with salt and pepper. Store, tightly covered, in the refrigerator for up to 2 days.

Souk Food

Kasbah (or Casbah) is a word that came into English in the late 19th century. Translated (from Arabic) it meant citadel and generally came to include a walled area surrounding a citadel. The Medina quarter is an old Arab quarter found in many North African cities. A souk, or market, is usually situated very close to the Kasbah or Medina. Dating back thousands of years, the souk may consist of open-air stalls surrounding an enclosed structure or it may just be a huge covered hall with aisles of stalls. Among the jumble of carts, pedestrians and wares on display, one finds everything from fresh herbs, meats, fish, fruits, vegetables, spices, carpets and housewares. Like street food anywhere in the world, souk food is delicious, easy to eat out of hand and convenient.

In the souk, one might stop for a vegetable or lamb kebab, or a sweet or savory pastry. Fresh juices (including pomegranate and orange), mint teas and strong Turkish coffees are abundant. My recipes here are not meant to be a direct translation of authentic souk food; rather they are a representation of the wide range of products and flavors that abound in these colorful, local, seasonal markets.

Almond and Herb-Stuffed Mushrooms

Makes 16 large mushroom caps

Use any large, fleshy mushroom, such as portobello for these tasty bites.

- **Preheat oven to 375°F (190°C)**
- **Baking sheet, lightly oiled**

| 16 | large mushrooms | 16 |
| 1 cup | Almond-Herb Filling (page 161) | 250 mL |

1. Remove, trim and finely chop mushroom stems. Set aside. Arrange mushroom caps, hollow side up, on prepared baking sheet.

2. In a small bowl, combine Almond-Herb Filling with reserved mushroom stems. Spoon about 2 tbsp (30 mL) of the filling into mushroom caps. Bake in preheated oven for 12 to 15 minutes or until filling is bubbly.

Almond-Herb Filling

Makes 1 cup (250 mL)

This almond and herb filling is one of several that can be used to stuff mushrooms and other vegetables, such as zucchini, bell peppers, tomatoes, potatoes and eggplant.

¾ cup	Mediterranean Pesto (page 46)	175 mL
¼ cup	chopped almonds	60 mL
3 tbsp	freshly grated Parmesan cheese	45 mL
½ tsp	sea salt	2 mL

1. In a small bowl, combine pesto, almonds, cheese and salt. Stir well.

Artichokes in Mediterranean Dressing

Makes 4 servings

The smoky flavor of the chipotle chiles complements the rather bland artichoke. Use this dish as a flavor-spike for tagines or to stuff peppers, eggplants, tomatoes or zucchini. As an appetizer, serve over torn fresh spinach, mesclun, watercress or other fresh greens.

Variation

Use hearts of palm in place of the artichoke hearts.

1	can (14 oz/398 mL) artichoke hearts (8 whole hearts), drained and rinsed	1
2	dried or canned chipotle chiles, thinly sliced	2
½ cup	Mediterranean Dressing (page 196)	125 mL
2 cups	torn mixed salad greens	500 mL

1. Cut artichoke hearts into quarters. In a bowl, combine artichokes and chile slices. Add dressing and toss to coat. Cover and refrigerate for 1 to 2 hours or overnight.

2. Bring artichokes to room temperature before serving. Divide greens evenly among 4 small salad plates. Spoon equal portions of artichoke mixture over greens. Serve immediately.

Cheese-Stuffed Eggplant Rolls

**Makes
4 servings**

The traditional way to make this Middle Eastern delicacy is to bread and deep-fry stuffed eggplant "sandwiches" but I prefer to skip the last steps and serve this lighter version warm or at room temperature.

Variation

Arrange stuffed eggplant rolls in a lightly greased 11- by 7-inch (28 by 18 cm) baking dish. Cover with 2 cups (500 mL) tomato sauce. Bake in preheated 350°F (180°C) oven for 20 to 30 minutes or until sauce is bubbly and rolls are heated through. Serve warm with rice or couscous for a light meal.

**Makes 1½ cups
(375 mL)**

- **Preheat oven to 375°F (190°C)**
- **2 baking sheets, lightly oiled**

2	long thin eggplants, ends trimmed	2
3 tbsp	salt	45 mL
3 tbsp	avocado or olive oil (approx.)	45 mL
1½ cups	Cheese Filling (see below)	375 mL

1. Slice eggplants lengthwise ⅛ inch (3 mm) thick. Place one layer in a large colander and sprinkle slices with salt. Repeat until all eggplant slices have been salted. Leave to drain for 1 hour. Rinse and pat dry.

2. Place eggplant slices on prepared baking sheets in a single layer, working in batches as necessary. Brush lightly with oil. Bake in preheated oven for 7 to 10 minutes or until lightly browned. Remove from oven, flip slices over and bake for another 3 minutes to brown the other side. Using tongs, lift slices from pan and transfer to drain on paper towels. Repeat with remaining slices.

3. Place 1 tbsp (15 mL) of the filling on one end of an eggplant slice and roll eggplant around it. Continue until all slices are rolled. Serve warm or cover and refrigerate overnight and reheat in a 350°F (180°C) oven for 10 minutes or until warmed through.

Cheese Filling

1 cup	Yogurt Cheese (page 155)	250 mL
4 oz	reduced-fat cream cheese	125 g
2	cloves garlic, minced	2
1 tsp	Moroccan Cinnamon Spice Blend (page 47) or store-bought garam masala	5 mL
1	egg, lightly beaten	1
2 tbsp	chopped fresh cilantro leaves	30 mL

1. In a bowl, combine Yogurt Cheese, cream cheese, garlic, spice blend, egg and cilantro. Stir to mix well.

Dukkah

Makes 2½ cups (625 mL)

This loose, dry mixture of chopped nuts and spices is crushed, not powdered or ground to a paste. In the Middle East, it is usually eaten as a snack with bread dipped in avocado or olive oil, or served at breakfast or any other time throughout the day. Each family has a slightly different version. The amounts here may be doubled or tripled.

1 cup	sesame seeds	250 mL
3 tbsp	coriander seeds	45 mL
2 tbsp	cumin seeds	30 mL
1 cup	unsalted dry roasted peanuts	250 mL
1 tsp	salt, or to taste	5 mL

1. In the bottom of a small tagine, spice wok or skillet over medium heat, toast sesame seeds, stirring constantly, for 1 to 2 minutes, until pale brown. Be careful not to burn the seeds. Transfer to a bowl and let cool.

2. In the same small tagine, spice wok or skillet, combine coriander and cumin. Toast over medium-high heat for 1 to 2 minutes or until lightly colored and fragrant. Remove from direct heat just as the seeds pop; do not let the spices smoke and burn. Let cool.

3. In a mortar (using pestle) or small electric grinder, pound or grind toasted spices until coarse or finely ground. Add sesame seeds and peanuts and pound or pulse until chopped fine. The texture should resemble coarse sand but not a paste. Tip into a small bowl and stir in salt, adding it to taste.

4. Store and label in a clean jar with lid in the refrigerator or cool, dark place for up to 2 months.

Dolmades

Dolmades — from the Arabic word, *dolma*, meaning "something stuffed" — are delicate parcels made by wrapping a variety of ingredients in grape leaves (also called vine leaves). Canned grape leaves packed in brine are available in specialty food stores.

8 oz	grape leaves in brine, drained and rinsed (see Tip, right)	250 g
5 tbsp	avocado or olive oil, divided	75 mL
3	green onions, sliced	3
¼ cup	finely chopped walnuts	60 mL
¼ tsp	ground cinnamon	1 mL
½ tsp	sea salt	2 mL
½ cup	long-grain white rice	125 mL
3 cups	vegetable broth or water, divided	750 mL
½ tsp	grated lemon zest	2 mL
2 tbsp	freshly squeezed lemon juice	30 mL
¼ cup	fresh green peas	60 mL
¼ cup	coarsely chopped fresh asparagus tips	60 mL
1 cup	Aïoli (page 149)	250 mL

1. Separate and select 20 to 30 of the best grape leaves. Soak in warm water for 30 minutes. Rinse and pat dry. Trim stems if necessary. Line the bottom of a large saucepan with 5 or 6 remaining grape leaves.

2. Meanwhile, in a skillet, heat 2 tbsp (30 mL) of the oil over medium heat. Add green onions and cook, stirring occasionally, for 4 minutes or until soft. Add walnuts and cook, stirring frequently, for 2 minutes. Stir in cinnamon, salt and rice. Cook, stirring occasionally, for 1 minute.

3. Add ¾ cup (175 mL) of the vegetable broth, lemon zest and juice and stir well. Bring to a boil over high heat. Cover, reduce heat and simmer for 10 minutes. Stir in peas and asparagus. Cover and let cool. Rice and vegetables will be only partially cooked at this point.

4. Lay out one grape leaf, vein side facing up and with stem end closest to you. Place 1 tbsp (15 mL) of the rice filling in the center of the leaf. Fold the stem end up over the filling. Neatly fold in the edges of both sides of the leaf. Roll the parcel toward the tip to finish the cigar-shaped wrap. Repeat with the remaining leaves and filling. Dolmades may be made up to this point and stored tightly wrapped in the refrigerator for up to 2 days. Bring to room temperature before steaming.

Tip

If you have fresh grape leaves, choose 25 or 30 small whole leaves. Blanch by cooking in a large saucepan of simmering water for 1 or 2 minutes. Drain and pat dry. Line the bottom of a large saucepan with 5 or 6 remaining grape leaves. Continue with Step 2.

5. Arrange the rolled dolmades side by side, seam side down, in a single layer if possible in the prepared saucepan. Drizzle with remaining oil and pour over the remaining vegetable broth. Broth should cover the dolmades (add more broth if required). Bring to a boil over high heat. Cover, reduce heat and gently simmer for 1 hour or until rice is tender.

6. Using a slotted spoon, lift the dolmades out of the cooking liquid and let cool in a large colander. Serve warm or at room temperature and pass with Aïoli.

Hot and Spicy Chickpeas and Almonds

Makes 3 cups (750 mL)

In Berber kitchens (sometimes little more than an open fire pit), dried chickpeas were a staple that was easy to store and transport. The legumes extended the protein in vegetable tagine dishes and meant that less meat was needed. In the souk, they are hot and usually not accompanied by nuts, and if you prefer, simply omit the nuts in this recipe.

● **Medium tagine**

2 tbsp	avocado or olive oil	30 mL
1	onion, chopped	1
2	cloves garlic, chopped	2
1	fresh hot chile pepper, chopped	1
1 tbsp	La Kama Spice Blend (page 44)	15 mL
1	can (14 to 19 oz/398 to 540 mL) chickpeas, drained and rinsed, or 2 cups (500 mL) cooked chickpeas	1
1 cup	almonds	250 mL

1. In the bottom of a flameproof tagine, heat oil over medium heat. Add onion, garlic, chile pepper and spice blend and cook, stirring, for 5 minutes. Stir in chickpeas and almonds. Cook, stirring frequently, for 7 to 10 minutes or until chickpeas and nuts are lightly toasted. Serve hot.

Roasted Red Peppers and Goat Cheese

Makes 2 cups (500 mL)

Use this as a warm dip for raw vegetables, pita points or crackers.

- **Small tagine**
- **Preheat oven to 350°F (180°C)**

2 cups	Roasted Red Peppers (page 51)	500 mL
2 oz	creamy goat cheese, cut into 4 slices	60 g
1 tbsp	Moroccan Cinnamon Spice Blend (page 47)	15 mL

1. Tip roasted peppers into the bottom of a small tagine. Heat over low heat until bubbling.

2. Place cheese slices on top of the peppers. Cover with tagine lid and simmer for 5 to 7 minutes or until cheese is melted. Sprinkle spice blend over cheese and serve warm.

Pan-Seared Artichokes with Pomegranate Molasses

Makes 4 servings

If you have never worked with fresh artichokes, they take just a bit of work to prepare, but are so much better than those in a jar or can. Save all the trimmings except the hairy choke (inner core) to use in vegetable stock.

● **Medium tagine**

	Juice of 1 lemon	
4	large artichokes	4
4 tbsp	avocado or olive oil, divided	60 mL
3	cloves garlic, slivered	3
	Sea salt and freshly ground black pepper	
1/4 cup	Pomegranate Molasses (page 172) or store-bought	60 mL
1/2 cup	Green Tomato and Apple Jam (page 152) or Mango Chutney (page 171)	125 mL

1. Prepare artichokes: Pour lemon juice into a large bowl and set aside. Working with one artichoke at a time, snap off the dark-green outer leaves, leaving the pale, tender inner leaves on the stem. Trim off all but 1 inch (2.5 cm) of the stem. Trim away the top third of the artichoke leaves. Use a paring knife to peel away the tough outer layer of the stem and to remove the base of the leaves. Cut the artichoke in half and half again. Trim away and discard the hairy choke and any thorny inner leaves of each quarter. As the artichokes are cut and trimmed, toss the quarters into the bowl with the lemon juice.

2. Add 2 tbsp (30 mL) of the oil to the bowl and toss to coat the artichoke quarters. In the bottom of a flameproof tagine, heat remaining oil over medium heat. Using tongs, add artichokes to tagine and arrange them with one cut side down. Reserve lemon juice and oil. Cook for 2 to 3 minutes or until browned on the one edge.

3. Add garlic to tagine. Turn and cook artichoke wedges on the other edge for another 2 to 3 minutes or until browned. Turn artichokes onto their curved side. Season to taste with salt and pepper. Drizzle Pomegranate Molasses and the reserved lemon juice and oil over all. Cover, reduce heat to low and simmer for about 7 minutes or until artichokes are tender when pierced with the tip of a knife.

4. To serve, plate 4 wedges on each serving plate. Drizzle with reduced pan juices and spoon 2 tbsp (30 mL) Green Tomato and Apple Jam onto the plate.

Anise Marinade

Makes ⅔ cup (150 mL)

Delicately licorice flavored from the fennel seeds and Pernod, this sauce is very nice for marinating fish, seafood and chicken destined for a tagine or the grill. Allow meat to marinate at least one hour or as long as overnight.

3 tbsp	Anise Seasoning (page 38) or fennel seeds, crushed	45 mL
2 tsp	coriander seeds, crushed	10 mL
⅓ cup	avocado or olive oil	75 mL
¼ cup	freshly squeezed lemon juice	60 mL
3 tbsp	Pernod or anise liquor, optional	45 mL
3 tbsp	white wine vinegar	45 mL

1. In a shallow bowl, combine seasoning and coriander seeds. Using a fork, whisk in oil until combined. Add lemon juice, Pernod, if using, and vinegar and stir until well mixed.

Date Molasses

Makes 2 cups (500 mL)

It has tang and isn't as sweet or as thick as brown rice syrup, but this pantry staple can be used as a less expensive alternative in most recipes.

● Blender

4 cups	apple or orange juice	1 L
1 cup	chopped pitted dates	250 mL
2 tbsp	freshly squeezed lemon juice	30 mL
2 tbsp	organic cane sugar crystals	30 mL
2 tsp	chopped pitted tamarind	10 mL

1. In a heavy-bottomed saucepan, combine apple juice, dates, lemon juice, sugar crystals and tamarind. Bring to a gentle boil over medium-high heat, stirring until sugar is dissolved. Reduce heat and keep gently simmering for about 1 hour or until thick and syrupy. Liquid should be reduced by at least one half. Let cool.

2. Using a blender, process date molasses until smooth. Store in an airtight container in the refrigerator for up to 1 month.

Peach Rose Sauce

Makes 2½ cups (625 mL)

Serve this pretty sauce chilled and use as you would a jam, with fruit or cheese. Alternatively, heat and drizzle it over vegetable or chicken tagines.

Tip
Use organic rose petals, not from florist shops.

Variation
Use orange water or apple juice in place of the rose water.

3	peaches, peeled and coarsely chopped	3
1 cup	pitted fresh apricots, quartered	250 mL
3 tbsp	rose water	45 mL
2 tbsp	Date Molasses (above) or brown rice syrup	30 mL
¼ cup	fresh rose petals, optional (see Tip, left)	60 mL

1. In a large saucepan, combine peaches, apricots, rose water and molasses. Cover and bring to a gentle boil over medium heat. Reduce heat and gently simmer for 15 minutes or until apricots are soft. Stir in rose petals, if using. Serve warm or refrigerate until chilled. Store, tightly covered, in the refrigerator for up to 3 days.

Mango Chutney

Makes 12 cups (3 L)

Choose firm, ripe, unblemished fruit for this versatile condiment. Use it with vegetable or meat tagines, stirred into yogurt as a dip, to accompany cheeses after dinner or with breakfast egg dishes.

Tip

Store cooled and labeled jars in a cold place for up to 6 months. Chutney will keep, tightly covered, in the refrigerator for up to 5 days.

Variation

Substitute peaches and plums for any of the fruit.

- **Freezer bags or six 2-cup (500 mL) preserving jars and lids, sterilized**

1 lb	mangos	500 g
1 lb	apricots	500 g
1 lb	nectarines	500 g
1 cup	raisins	250 mL
½ cup	freshly squeezed lime juice	125 mL
2 tbsp	avocado or olive oil	30 mL
2 cups	thinly sliced onions	500 mL
1¼ cups	white wine vinegar	300 mL
¼ cup	chicken broth	60 mL
¾ cup	organic cane sugar crystals	175 mL
½ cup	chopped preserved stem ginger	125 mL
1 tbsp	Ras el Hanout (page 50) or store-bought	15 mL
1 tbsp	Moroccan Cinnamon Spice Blend (page 47)	15 mL
1 tbsp	ground turmeric	15 mL
2 tsp	sea salt	10 mL

1. Peel mangos, apricots and nectarines. Remove stones and cut flesh into ½-inch (1 cm) pieces. Transfer to a large bowl and combine with raisins and lime juice. Set aside.

2. In a large nonreactive saucepan, heat oil over medium-low heat. Add onions and cook, stirring often, for 10 minutes. Stir in fruit and their juices, vinegar and chicken broth. Increase heat to medium-high and bring to a gentle boil. Boil, stirring often, for 3 minutes.

3. Stir in sugar, ginger, ras el hanout, Moroccan Cinnamon Spice Blend, turmeric and sea salt. Reduce heat and simmer gently, stirring occasionally, for 15 minutes or until fruit is soft but not puréed.

4. If freezing, cover and let cool. Spoon into 2-cup (500 mL) freezer bags and label. If preserving in canning jars, spoon hot fruit into hot mason jars, removing air bubbles and leaving a ½-inch (1 cm) headspace. Cover with 2-piece canning lids, securing the band by hand. Process using the boiling water method for 15 minutes. Refrigerate any jars with lids that do not "snap" to indicate a seal.

Pomegranate Molasses

Makes 2 cups (500 mL)

Very common in Middle Eastern cooking, this slightly tart syrupy condiment is used in many Turkish and Moroccan dishes. It is often available in Middle Eastern specialty food stores but this recipe is so easy to make and store, it can become a pantry staple.

● **1 pint (2 cup/500 mL) canning jar and lid**

4 cups	pomegranate juice	1 L
½ cup	organic cane sugar crystals	125 mL
¼ cup	freshly squeezed lemon juice	60 mL

1. In a heavy-bottomed saucepan, combine pomegranate juice, sugar crystals and lemon juice. Bring to a gentle boil over medium-high heat, stirring until sugar is dissolved. Reduce heat and keep gently simmering for about 1 hour or until thick and syrupy. Liquid should be reduced by at least one half. Pour the hot liquid into canning jar before cooling. Cap and let cool completely.

2. Store in the refrigerator for up to 2 months.

Tomato Sauce

Makes 2 cups (500 mL)

Oregano is sometimes called the "pizza herb" because it goes so well with tomatoes. Fresh oregano — *O. x majoricum* — is the best variety for tomato sauce. It and fresh basil are the keys to this great-tasting tomato sauce.

2 lbs	ripe tomatoes	1 kg
2 tbsp	avocado or olive oil	30 mL
1	red onion, finely chopped	1
4	large cloves garlic, minced	4
2 tbsp	chopped fresh oregano	30 mL
1 tbsp	chopped fresh parsley	15 mL
½ tsp	sea salt	2 mL
	Freshly ground black pepper	
3 tbsp	chopped fresh basil	45 mL

1. In a large pot of boiling water, blanch tomatoes for 30 seconds. Plunge into cold water and slip skins off. Cut in half, gently squeeze and discard seeds. Coarsely chop flesh and set aside.

2. In a large skillet or saucepan, heat oil over medium heat. Stir in red onion and cook, stirring, for about 7 minutes or until soft. Do not brown. Add garlic and cook, stirring, for 2 to 3 minutes or until fragrant.

3. Add tomatoes and oregano and simmer, stirring occasionally, for 10 minutes or until sauce is thickened slightly. Stir in parsley, salt, and pepper to taste and simmer, stirring occasionally, for another 10 minutes or until sauce has reached the desired thickness. Stir in basil and serve immediately.

Walnut Sauce

Makes 2 cups (500 mL)

This makes a fairly thick sauce that can be used as a thickener for tagine dishes, a topping for vegetables or in lasagna, or as a spread or dip.

Tip

To make a thinner sauce: In Step 3, with motor of food processor running, slowly add more water through opening in feed tube until desired consistency is achieved.

● **Food processor**

1 cup	coarsely chopped walnuts, divided	250 mL
1 cup	warm water, divided	250 mL
1	clove garlic	1
1	piece (1 inch/2.5 cm) candied ginger	1
1 tbsp	fresh rosemary needles	15 mL
2	slices whole-grain bread, torn into chunks	2
2 tbsp	freshly squeezed lemon juice	30 mL
2 tsp	avocado or olive oil	10 mL
2 tsp	Dijon mustard	10 mL
1/4 tsp	salt, optional	1 mL
	Freshly ground black pepper	

1. In a small bowl, cover 1/2 cup (125 mL) of the walnuts with 1/2 cup (125 mL) of the water. Set aside for at least 30 minutes or for up to 6 hours.

2. Meanwhile, chop remaining walnuts slightly more than coarse but not fine. Set aside.

3. Drain and rinse soaked walnuts and place in food processor. Add garlic, ginger and rosemary and pulse to chop and combine. Add bread, lemon juice, oil, mustard, salt, if using, and pepper to taste and pulse to combine. With motor running, add remaining water through opening in feed tube. Stop and scrape down sides of the bowl. Pulse until the mixture is very smooth. Taste and add more mustard, lemon juice or salt, if required.

4. Transfer purée to a small bowl and stir in reserved walnuts. Use immediately or store, tightly covered, in the refrigerator for up to 4 days.

Sides and Salads

Sides

Salads

continued...

Beet Tagine

Makes 4 to 6 servings

Slightly sweet, this colorful side dish tagine is often enjoyed by ardent beet haters.

● **Medium or large tagine**

4	medium beets	4
2 tbsp	avocado or olive oil	30 mL
1	onion, chopped	1
2 tsp	Ground Moroccan Spice Blend (page 44) or store bought garam masala	10 mL
½	fennel bulb, sliced	½
½ cup	chicken broth	125 mL
⅓ cup	apple juice	75 mL
1	apple, quartered	1
¼ cup	sliced dried apricots	60 mL
2 tbsp	balsamic vinegar	30 mL
1 to 2 tbsp	honey, optional	15 to 30 mL
	Salt and freshly ground black pepper	

1. Trim and scrub beets. Cut into wedges.

2. In the bottom of a flameproof tagine, heat oil over medium heat. Add onion and spice blend and cook, stirring, for 5 minutes or until soft. Add beets, fennel, broth and apple juice and bring to a boil. Cover, reduce heat to low and simmer for about 35 minutes or until beets are tender.

3. Stir in apple, apricots, vinegar and honey to taste, if using. Simmer, uncovered, for about 7 minutes or until apples are soft and sauce is reduced slightly. Season to taste with salt and pepper. Serve warm.

Braised Swiss Chard with Almond Butter Sauce

The nut sauce here is thinned with water so as not to overpower the greens. Make the sauce first so it is ready to drizzle over the greens as soon as they are wilted. Use less water in the sauce if you plan to serve it with cooked vegetables. Swiss chard is not as delicate as many other greens but when cooked in this manner, it is tender and delicate in taste.

Tip

Be sure to use a high quality, freshly made nut butter that contains no hydrogenated oils, sugar or preservatives.

Variations

Use freshly ground peanut butter or cashew butter in place of almond butter.

Substitute one or a mixture of mustard, beet or turnip greens, or spinach for the Swiss chard and adjust cooking time to suit the greens, 1 to 1½ minutes or until tender.

● **Warmed serving bowl or platter**

Almond Butter Sauce

½ cup	freshly ground almond butter (see Tip, left)	125 mL
¼ cup	freshly squeezed lemon juice	60 mL
2 tbsp	tamari or soy sauce	30 mL
2 tsp	freshly grated gingerroot	10 mL
⅓ cup	warm water	75 mL

Braised Swiss Chard

1	bunch Swiss chard or kale leaves	1
2 tbsp	avocado or olive oil	30 mL
1	onion, coarsely chopped	1
2	cloves garlic, finely chopped	2
1 cup	Almond Butter Sauce (see recipe, above)	250 mL
¼ cup	raisins	60 mL
¼ cup	coarsely chopped natural almonds	60 mL

1. *Almond Butter Sauce:* In a small bowl, combine almond butter, lemon juice, tamari and ginger. Gradually stir in warm water until sauce reaches a creamy consistency.

2. *Braised Swiss Chard:* Remove and discard tough center stem from Swiss chard leaves. Coarsely chop leaves and tender stems (to make 6 cups/1.5 L). In a large saucepan, bring 2 quarts (2 L) water to boil over high heat. Drop leaves and chopped stems into water. Reduce heat and simmer for 1 to 2 minutes or just until tender. Drain and rinse with cold water.

3. In a large skillet, heat oil over medium heat. Add onion and cook, stirring, for 5 minutes. Stir in garlic and cook for another 2 minutes. Add blanched Swiss chard to the skillet and toss to mix with onion and garlic. Transfer to warmed serving bowl or platter and drizzle with Almond Butter Sauce. Sprinkle raisins and nuts over top. Serve immediately.

Cauliflower Tagine

**Makes
4 servings**

Cauliflower is super in
this easy vegetable side
dish, but you can use
carrots, pumpkin, turnip
or rutabaga.

● **Medium tagine**

¾ cup	dried split green peas	175 mL
2 cups	water	500 mL
2 tbsp	avocado or olive oil	30 mL
1	onion, chopped	1
1 tbsp	Turmeric Spice Paste (page 53) or curry powder	15 mL
1	small cauliflower, cut into florets	1
½ cup	chicken broth	125 mL
1 cup	chopped raw almonds or walnuts	250 mL

1. In a saucepan, cover split peas with water. Bring to a boil over medium heat. Cover, reduce heat and simmer for 15 to 20 minutes or until peas are tender. Drain and set aside.

2. Meanwhile, in the bottom of a flameproof tagine, heat oil over medium heat. Add onion and spice paste and cook, stirring, for 5 minutes. Add cauliflower and cook, stirring constantly, for 1 minute. Add broth and bring to a boil. Cover, reduce heat and simmer for 10 minutes or until cauliflower is tender. Stir in cooked peas and heat through. Sprinkle almonds over top. Serve immediately.

Basil and Roasted Pepper Couscous

**Makes
4 servings**

Chipotle is the name given to jalapeño peppers that have been smoked and dried. The thick flesh is free of peel and lends a distinctly smoky flavor to dishes. They are most commonly available canned in adobo sauce.

Variation

Substitute 1 cup (250 mL) chopped fresh red bell peppers for the roasted red pepper slices and cook with onion in Step 2.

● **Small or medium tagine**

1 cup	chicken broth or water	250 mL
1 cup	instant couscous	250 mL
2 tbsp	avocado or olive oil	30 mL
1 cup	chopped red onion	250 mL
2	cloves garlic, finely chopped	2
1 tsp	Ground Moroccan Spice Blend (page 44) or store-bought garam masala	5 mL
2 cups	Roasted Red Peppers (page 51), coarsely chopped	500 mL
¼ cup	chopped drained canned chipotle peppers	60 mL
1 tbsp	rice vinegar	15 mL
½ tsp	salt	2 mL

1. In a saucepan, bring broth to a boil over high heat. Stir in couscous, cover and remove from heat. Let stand for 5 minutes. Fluff with a fork.

2. Meanwhile, in the bottom of a flameproof tagine, heat oil over medium heat. Add red onion and garlic and cook, stirring, for 7 minutes or until soft. Add spice blend, red peppers, chipotle peppers, vinegar and salt and cook, stirring constantly, for 2 minutes. Toss with couscous and serve immediately.

Herbed Couscous

**Makes
4 servings**

Having prepared pesto on hand makes this an easy accompaniment for tagine dishes.

1 cup	chicken broth or water	250 mL
1 cup	instant couscous	250 mL
¼ cup	Coriander Pesto (page 41) or Mediterranean Pesto (page 46)	60 mL

1. In a saucepan, bring broth to a boil over high heat. Stir in couscous, cover and remove from heat. Let stand for 5 minutes.

2. Fluff couscous with a fork and stir in pesto.

Buttered Almond Couscous

Makes 4 servings

Toasting the almonds in the cinnamon blend adds to their flavor.

● **Small or medium tagine**

1 cup	chicken broth or water	250 mL
1 cup	instant couscous	250 mL
2 tbsp	butter	30 mL
¼ cup	raw almonds	60 mL
2 tsp	Ground Moroccan Spice Blend (page 44) or store-bought garam masala	10 mL

1. In a saucepan, bring broth to a boil over high heat. Stir in couscous, cover and remove from heat. Let stand for 5 minutes. Fluff with a fork.

2. Meanwhile, in the bottom of a flameproof tagine, heat butter over medium heat. Add almonds and spice blend and toast, stirring frequently, for 4 to 6 minutes or until almonds are light brown. Toss with couscous and serve immediately.

Couscous

Couscous is a Middle Eastern staple that was (and still is by some home cooks) made by hand by rolling moistened semolina grains in durum wheat flour. The tiny pellets are traditionally steamed in a *couscoussière*. Hand rolled (or machine made) authentic couscous is usually only available in specialty food and Middle Eastern stores, and it takes about 15 to 20 minutes to steam.

More common in North America is "instant" couscous that is softened by letting it stand in very hot (just boiled) water or broth, usually for 5 minutes (check instructions on the package). The recipes in this section use this instant couscous.

Moroccan Sweet Potato Soup

**Makes
4 servings**

The taste combination of the distinctly Moroccan spice blend and the sweet potatoes along with the coconut milk makes this complex and mildly spicy soup a great starter for a lunch meal or for a soup-salad combo.

2 tbsp	avocado or olive oil	30 mL
1 cup	chopped onion	250 mL
1 tbsp	Bahrat Spice Blend (page 39) or store-bought garam masala	15 mL
2	sweet potatoes, peeled and cut into large dice	2
1 cup	chopped carrot	250 mL
3 cups	vegetable broth	750 mL
¼ cup	chopped raisins	60 mL
1 tsp	salt	5 mL
1	can (14 oz/400 mL) coconut milk	1
½ cup	Drained Yogurt (page 183)	125 mL
¼ cup	chopped red bell pepper	60 mL

1. In a large saucepan, heat oil over medium heat. Add onion and spice blend and cook, stirring, for 6 minutes. Stir in sweet potatoes and carrot. Cook, stirring constantly, for 3 minutes.

2. Stir in broth. Increase heat to medium-high and bring to a boil. Reduce heat and simmer, stirring occasionally, for 15 minutes. Add raisins and salt. Cook for 5 minutes or until all vegetables are soft. Remove from heat.

3. Using a potato masher, roughly mash sweet potato mixture. Stir in coconut milk and yogurt. Return to medium-high heat and heat through. Ladle soup into 4 bowls. Float 1 tbsp (15 mL) chopped red pepper on top of each bowl. Serve immediately.

Drained Yogurt

Makes 2 cups (500 mL) lightly drained or 1⅔ cups (400 mL) yogurt cheese

Draining yogurt makes it thicker. The longer you let the yogurt drain, the thicker will be the result and if you let it drain overnight, it will resemble soft cream cheese. This is what we mean by the term "yogurt cheese."

2 cups	plain yogurt	500 mL

1. Line a strainer with cheesecloth. Set the strainer over a bowl large enough to catch the liquid. Place yogurt in strainer and let drain over the bowl in the refrigerator for 10 minutes for a thick yogurt and as long as overnight for yogurt cheese. Discard liquid.

Spiced Lemon Tagine Rice

Makes 6 servings

Of course you can make this delicately spiced rice using a saucepan, but the tagine keeps the rice moist and once it is cooked, it will stay hot in the tagine longer.

● **Medium tagine**

2 tbsp	avocado or olive oil	30 mL
1	onion, chopped	1
1 tsp	cumin seeds	5 mL
2	cloves garlic, finely chopped	2
1	carrot, grated	1
½ tsp	ground nutmeg	2 mL
½ tsp	ground cinnamon	2 mL
1½ cups	basmati rice	375 mL
2½ cups	vegetable broth	625 mL
1 tsp	grated lemon zest	5 mL
¼ cup	freshly squeezed lemon juice	60 mL

1. In the bottom of a flameproof tagine, heat oil over medium heat. Add onion and cumin and cook, stirring, for 5 minutes. Add garlic, carrot, nutmeg and cinnamon and cook, stirring, for 2 minutes. Add rice and lightly toast, stirring frequently, for 2 minutes.

2. Add vegetable broth and lemon juice and bring to a boil. Cover, reduce heat to low and cook for 15 to 20 minutes or until rice is tender and liquid is absorbed. Remove lid, fluff the rice with a fork and stir in lemon zest.

Sweet Potato Tagine

Makes 4 to 6 servings

Using sweet potatoes in place of regular spuds increases the vitamin A.

Variation

Add ¼ cup (60 mL) any of the following: nuts or seeds, flaked coconut or raisins.

● **Medium or large tagine**

4	medium sweet potatoes, scrubbed and quartered	4
3 tbsp	avocado or olive oil	45 mL
1	leek, white and tender green parts, sliced	1
1	onion, chopped	1
1 tbsp	Ras el Hanout (page 50) or store-bought	15 mL
½ cup	chicken broth	125 mL
1 tbsp	liquid honey	15 mL

1. In a large saucepan, cover sweet potatoes with water. Bring to a boil over high heat. Reduce heat and simmer for 20 minutes or until tender. Drain, let cool and remove skins. Cut into large dice and set aside.

2. Meanwhile, in the bottom of a flameproof tagine, heat oil over medium heat. Add leek, onion and ras el hanout and cook, stirring, for 7 minutes or until soft. Stir in broth and honey and bring to a boil. Reduce heat and simmer, stirring occasionally, for 10 to 12 minutes or until liquid is slightly reduced.

3. Add sweet potatoes and toss to coat with leek mixture. Serve warm or at room temperature.

Tabbouleh

**Makes
4 servings**

Fresh tasting and nutty, this fast and delicious grain dish may be served as an appetizer or as a main dish accompaniment. Omit the tomatoes and use it as a stuffing for vegetables and fish. Garnish it with any of the following to create a light lunch: olives, sliced avocado, artichoke hearts, cooked tuna slivers, cooked lentils, hard-cooked eggs or grated cheese.

Variation

Instant couscous is widely available and only requires a few minutes of soaking. It may be used in place of bulgur in this recipe. Follow package directions for soaking 1 cup (250 mL) couscous, substituting vegetable or mushroom broth for the water called for. Follow Steps 2 and 3 in the recipe.

1 cup	bulgur	250 mL
2½ cups	chicken broth	625 mL
1 cup	chopped fresh parsley	250 mL
½ cup	finely chopped onion	125 mL
¼ cup	finely chopped green onions	60 mL
¼ cup	chopped fresh mint	60 mL
2	tomatoes, seeded and coarsely chopped	2
¼ cup	avocado or olive oil	60 mL
3 tbsp	freshly squeezed lemon juice	45 mL
1 tbsp	Moroccan Cinnamon Spice Blend (page 47) or store-bought garam masala	15 mL
½ tsp	salt	2 mL
	Freshly ground black pepper	

1. In a saucepan, combine bulgur and broth. Cover and bring to a gentle simmer over medium heat. Reduce heat to low and cook for 20 to 25 minutes or until grain is soft but still chewy and liquid is absorbed. Remove from heat and let stand, covered, for 10 minutes.

2. Fluff with a fork and transfer to a serving tagine or large bowl. Stir in parsley, onion, green onions, mint and tomatoes. Toss to combine.

3. In a small bowl, whisk together oil, lemon juice, spice blend and salt. Toss with bulgur. Season to taste with pepper. Add more seasoning, lemon juice or salt, if required. Serve at room temperature.

Tomato, Thyme and Zucchini Bulgur

Makes 4 to 6 servings

Bulgur is a processed grain made from wheat berries that have been steamed, dried and crushed. It comes in various textures — fine, medium and coarse — and cooks very quickly because of the processing. The texture of bulgur you use depends more on your personal preference, what is available to you as well as what effect you wish to achieve. For example, with this recipe, I might prefer to use a coarse bulgur, but any of the textures will work.

2 tbsp	avocado or olive oil	30 mL
1	onion, chopped	1
1	zucchini, chopped	1
2	cloves garlic, finely chopped	2
1	can (28 oz/796 mL) stewed tomatoes with juice, chopped	1
1 cup	chicken broth or water	250 mL
2 tbsp	chopped fresh oregano	30 mL
1 tbsp	fresh thyme leaves	15 mL
1 tsp	Bahrat Spice Blend (page 39) or store-bought garam masala	5 mL
2/3 cup	bulgur	150 mL

1. In a saucepan, heat oil over medium-high heat. Add onion and cook, stirring occasionally, for 3 minutes or until slightly softened. Add zucchini and garlic and cook, stirring frequently, for 1 minute. Add tomatoes with juice and broth and bring to a boil. Stir in oregano, thyme, spice blend and bulgur. Cover, reduce heat and simmer for 20 to 25 minutes or until bulgur is tender and all or most of the liquid has been absorbed.

Tunisian Carrot Tagine

**Makes
4 servings**

Colorful, lightly spiced and delicious, this recipe is a slightly different tagine dish because the cooked vegetables are tossed in marinated feta, which could also be used with couscous.

● **Medium tagine**

1 tbsp	avocado or olive oil	15 mL
1 cup	chopped onions	250 mL
1 tbsp	Tunisian Five Spices (page 54)	15 mL
4 cups	diced carrots	1 L
¾ cup	water or chicken broth (approx.)	175 mL
6 oz	feta cheese, drained	175 g
⅓ cup	olive oil	75 mL
¼ cup	chopped fresh parsley	60 mL
2 tbsp	white wine vinegar	30 mL
1	clove garlic, minced	1
1 tbsp	chopped fresh marjoram	15 mL
1 tsp	ground cumin	5 mL
¼ tsp	ground cinnamon	1 mL
¼ cup	plain yogurt	60 mL
½ cup	sliced black olives	125 mL

1. In the bottom of a flameproof tagine, heat oil over medium heat. Add onions and spice blend and cook, stirring, for 5 minutes. Add carrots and cook, stirring, for 2 minutes. Add water, just until it covers the vegetables. Cover, reduce heat to low and simmer for 10 to 12 minutes or until vegetables are tender-crisp. Drain.

2. Meanwhile, cut feta into small cubes and place in a large bowl. In a clean jar with tight-fitting lid, combine olive oil, parsley, vinegar, garlic, marjoram, cumin and cinnamon. Shake well to combine and pour over the feta. Cover and let stand, stirring occasionally, for at least 30 minutes.

3. Using a fork, stir yogurt into the feta and dressing. Add warm carrots and toss well. Divide salad among 4 plates and garnish with black olives.

Vegetable and Lentil Soup

**Makes
4 servings**

Easy to make, this soup
is hearty enough for
a light winter lunch
and the yogurt adds
a unique taste.

2 tbsp	Ground Moroccan Spice Blend (page 44)	30 mL
1 tbsp	avocado or olive oil	15 mL
1 tsp	toasted sesame oil	5 mL
1 cup	chopped onions	250 mL
4 cups	chicken or vegetable broth	1 L
1 cup	dried red or green lentils, rinsed and drained	250 mL
1 cup	chopped green cabbage	250 mL
1	zucchini, finely chopped	1
1	carrot, finely chopped	1
1	parsnip, finely chopped	1
1	stalk celery, finely chopped	1
	Salt and freshly ground black pepper	
1 cup	plain yogurt	250 mL
¼ cup	chopped fresh parsley, optional	60 mL

1. In a large saucepan, stir spice blend with avocado oil and sesame oil to make a paste. Heat gently over medium-low heat. Cook, stirring constantly, for 1 minute. Add onions and cook, stirring constantly, for 5 minutes.

2. Add broth and bring to a boil over high heat. Reduce heat, add lentils, cover and simmer for 45 minutes or until lentils are tender.

3. Add cabbage, zucchini, carrot, parsnip and celery. Cover and simmer, stirring occasionally, for 25 minutes. Season to taste with salt and pepper. Remove from heat and stir yogurt into soup. Ladle into soup bowls and garnish with parsley, if using.

Avocado and Sesame Salad

**Makes
4 servings**

Make this in summer
or winter because
avocados are in markets
year-round. Served
chilled or at room
temperature, it's easy
and fresh tasting as a
starter or as a side dish
for tagines.

¼ cup	avocado or olive oil	60 mL
2 tbsp	Pomegranate Molasses (page 172) or store-bought	30 mL
1 tbsp	tahini	15 mL
2 tsp	Ground Moroccan Spice Blend (page 44) or store-bought garam masala	10 mL
3	avocados	3
2 tbsp	freshly squeezed lemon juice	30 mL
1	small red onion, thinly sliced	1
½	fennel bulb, thinly sliced	½
1 cup	baby spinach leaves	250 mL
4 tbsp	sesame seeds	60 mL

1. In a jar with tight-fitting lid, combine oil, molasses, tahini and spice blend. Shake well to combine. Set aside.

2. Peel, pit and slice avocados into a bowl. Toss with lemon juice, red onion, fennel and spinach. Drizzle tahini dressing over top and toss to coat vegetables. Divide evenly among 4 plates and garnish each with 1 tbsp (15 mL) sesame seeds.

Beet and Feta Cheese Salad

**Makes
4 servings**

Pink and perfectly
seasoned, this salad is
pretty served over fresh,
tender spring greens.

4	beets, cooked and sliced	4
¼ cup	chopped red onion	60 mL
¼ cup	chopped fresh parsley	60 mL
¼ cup	chopped dates	60 mL
¼ cup	sliced figs	60 mL
3 tbsp	avocado or olive oil	45 mL
1 tbsp	rice vinegar	15 mL
1 tsp	fresh thyme leaves	5 mL
1 tsp	chopped fresh rosemary	5 mL
¼ cup	crumbled feta cheese	60 mL
¼ cup	slivered toasted almonds	60 mL

1. In a salad bowl, toss together beets, red onion, parsley, dates and figs.

2. In a small jar with a lid or small bowl, combine oil, vinegar, thyme and rosemary. Shake or whisk to mix well.

3. Pour dressing over salad ingredients. Toss gently to mix. Sprinkle with feta and almonds and serve immediately.

Chickpea, Potato and Chicken Salad

Makes 4 to 6 servings

Substantial and fresh tasting, this salad is a great dish for family and guests, and the big bonus is that it may be made a day in advance.

Tip

You can use leftover baked chicken for this recipe, but poaching helps retain the moisture in the meat.

To poach chicken: Place the trimmed breast in a pan with a mixture of half wine, half water — enough to cover. Add several sprigs of fresh parsley, 4 peppercorns, a bay leaf and a pinch of dried thyme. Bring to a boil over high heat. Cover, reduce heat and simmer gently on low to medium heat for about 20 minutes or until no longer pink inside. Drain and let cool. Chicken may be poached the day before, covered and refrigerated until ready to cube and add to the salad.

1 cup	mayonnaise	250 mL
1/4 cup	Coriander Pesto (page 41) or store-bought basil pesto	60 mL
1 tbsp	freshly squeezed lemon juice	15 mL
1 1/2 cups	Drained Yogurt (page 183)	375 mL
2 cups	cubed poached chicken breast (see Tip, left)	500 mL
1 cup	cubed cooked potatoes	250 mL
1 cup	chopped red bell pepper	250 mL
1	can (14 to 19 oz/398 to 540 mL) chickpeas, rinsed and drained, or 2 cups (500 mL) cooked chickpeas	1
1/2 cup	sliced black olives	125 mL
1/4 cup	capers, rinsed and drained	60 mL
1/4 cup	chopped red onion	60 mL
	Salt and freshly ground black pepper	

1. In a large bowl, combine mayonnaise and pesto. Stir in lemon juice and drained yogurt. Fold in chicken, potatoes, bell pepper, chickpeas, olives, capers and red onion. Cover and refrigerate for at least 3 hours or overnight to allow the flavors to mellow. Season with salt and pepper to taste.

Fattoush

**Makes
4 servings**

Every household and every café in North Africa has a personalized version of this fresh pepper and tomato salad, and each season brings different ingredients to be included so there is never one way of making it. Some variations are listed below, but use your own favorites to make this salad your own.

Tip

Serving suggestion: On a large round or oval platter, spread greens or cucumber. Arrange salad in a ring on the greens. Mound Bread Dressing in the center of the ring. Sprinkle cheese over salad. Serve immediately.

Variations

For the salad ingredients, roughly 4 cups (1 L) of mixed greens, legumes and vegetables will serve 4 people. Use any combination of the following:

- Sliced artichoke
- Chopped fresh parsley, mint or cilantro
- Cooked lentils, lima beans, flageolets or chickpeas
- Grated cabbage or root vegetables in winter
- 1 can (7 oz/210 g) tuna or salmon, drained, or ½ cup (125 mL) other cooked fresh water fish, flaked.

Bread Dressing

3 tbsp	freshly squeezed lemon juice, divided	45 mL
2 tbsp	water	30 mL
2	slices dry brown bread, cubed	2
3 tbsp	avocado or olive oil	45 mL
1	clove garlic, minced	1
1 tsp	crushed coriander seeds	5 mL
½ tsp	crushed caraway seeds	2 mL
¼ tsp	salt, or to taste	1 mL
¼ tsp	Harissa (page 45), optional	1 mL

Salad

2 cups	Roasted Red Peppers (page 51), sliced, or chopped red bell pepper	500 mL
2	tomatoes, coarsely chopped	2
2	green onions, thinly sliced on the diagonal	2
¼ cup	coarsely chopped pitted black olives	60 mL
2 tbsp	capers, rinsed and drained, optional	30 mL
2 tsp	grated lemon zest	10 mL
2 cups	mixed greens or thinly sliced cucumber	500 mL
½ cup	crumbled drained feta cheese	125 mL

1. *Bread Dressing:* In a bowl, mix 1 tbsp (15 mL) of the lemon juice with water. Stir in bread cubes. Cover and set aside to soften while making the salad (see Step 3).

2. When bread is soft, using a fork, whisk remaining 2 tbsp (30 mL) of lemon juice, oil, garlic, coriander, caraway, salt, and Harissa, if using, into softened bread cubes. Taste and adjust seasonings, if required. Cover and set aside until ready to use.

3. *Salad:* In a salad bowl, toss together roasted peppers, tomatoes, green onions, olives, capers, if using, and lemon zest to mix well.

4. Add dressing and toss to combine with salad ingredients or see Tip, left. Sprinkle cheese over salad. Serve immediately.

Fennel, Spinach and Oranges with Golden Ginger Dressing

Makes 4 servings

Fennel bulb lends a delicate anise flavor to the greens in this salad. Use as much fresh ginger as your taste dictates.

Golden Ginger Dressing

2 tbsp	avocado or olive oil	30 mL
2 tbsp	rice vinegar	30 mL
1 tbsp	tamari or soy sauce	15 mL
2 tsp	grated fresh gingerroot	10 mL
2 tsp	ground turmeric	10 mL
1 tsp	organic cane sugar crystals or brown sugar	5 mL
¼ tsp	hot pepper flakes	1 mL

Salad

2 cups	baby spinach leaves	500 mL
2	oranges, sectioned	2
½	fennel bulb, thinly sliced	½
½	red onion, thinly sliced	½

1. *Golden Ginger Dressing:* In a salad bowl, whisk together oil, vinegar, tamari, ginger, turmeric, sugar and hot pepper flakes.

2. *Salad:* Add spinach, oranges, fennel and red onion to dressing and toss to coat.

Grated Carrots with Dates and Walnuts

Makes 4 servings

A simple, raw and nutritious salad, this dish can become a staple in the winter when fresh carrots are still plentiful.

Variations

Add shredded apple or turnip.

Use raisins or dried cranberries in place of the dates.

Substitute other favorite nuts and seeds for the walnuts.

4	carrots, grated	4
2	green onions, thinly sliced diagonally	2
1/3 cup	chopped dates	75 mL
1/4 cup	coarsely chopped walnuts	60 mL
1/3 cup	Golden Ginger Dressing (page 194) or Mediterranean Dressing (page 196)	75 mL

1. In a large bowl, combine carrots, green onions, dates and walnuts. Toss with dressing to coat. Serve immediately.

Green Bean, Pistachio and Pomegranate Salad

Makes 4 servings

Fast, easy and great tasting, this salad can step in as an appetizer or accompaniment to either a meat or vegetable tagine dish. Serve it with whole grains or couscous for a light lunch. Do not be tempted to cook the beans for more than 3 minutes or their texture will soften too much.

Tip
Pomegranate seeds are available at Middle Eastern markets and specialty shops.

1 lb	green beans, cut into 2-inch (5 cm) pieces	500 g
½ cup	diced red onion	125 mL
1 cup	whole pistachio nuts	250 mL
1 cup	pomegranate seeds (see Tip, left)	250 mL
¼ cup	chopped green olives, optional	60 mL

Pomegranate Dressing

⅓ cup	avocado or olive oil	75 mL
3 tbsp	Pomegranate Molasses (page 172) or store-bought	45 mL
1 tbsp	chopped fresh parsley	15 mL

1. In a pot of boiling salted water, cook green beans for 3 minutes. Drain and rinse with cold water. Let cool to room temperature. In a bowl, combine green beans, red onion, pistachio nuts, pomegranate seeds, and olives, if using.

2. *Pomegranate Dressing:* Meanwhile, in a jar with a tight-fitting lid, combine oil, molasses and parsley. Shake well to combine and drizzle over salad.

Mediterranean Dressing

Makes ⅓ cup (75 mL)

Lemons and garlic are classic Mediterranean region ingredients. The light and zippy dressing complements other ingredients of the area such as olives, artichokes, legumes and red peppers.

3 tbsp	avocado or olive oil	45 mL
2 tbsp	freshly squeezed lemon juice	30 mL
1	clove garlic, minced	1
2	anchovy fillets, drained and chopped, optional	2
	Freshly ground black pepper	

1. In a jar with lid or small bowl, combine oil, lemon juice, garlic, anchovies, if using, and pepper to taste. Shake or whisk to mix well. Taste and add more lemon juice, if required.

Mediterranean Bean Salad

**Makes
4 servings**

Make this salad your own by adding your favorite vegetables. In the winter, 1 cup (250 mL) shredded cabbage or root vegetables add texture and vitamins. Summer squash or peas or beans, steamed just till they crunch, make great warm weather ingredients.

Variations

Substitute chopped nuts for the lentils but add just before serving. Chopped red or green bell pepper may replace the olives.

Add any of the following, 1 cup (250 mL) cooked green beans, 2 chopped hard-cooked eggs, 3 oz (90 g) drained, crumbled feta cheese, or ½ cup (125 mL) cherry tomato halves or 1 to 2 oz (30 to 60 g) of fresh cooked tuna or other cold water fish.

1	can (14 to 19 oz/398 to 540 mL) broad beans or cannellini beans, rinsed and drained, or 2 cups (500 mL) cooked navy beans or Great Northern beans	1
½ cup	cooked red lentils	125 mL
½ cup	coarsely chopped drained canned artichoke halves or hearts of palm	125 mL
½ cup	diced red onion	125 mL
¼ cup	chopped fresh parsley	60 mL
¼ cup	coarsely chopped black or green olives	60 mL
¼ cup	Mediterranean Dressing (page 196)	60 mL

1. In a large bowl, combine beans, lentils, artichokes, red onion, parsley and olives. Toss with dressing. Cover and let stand for at least 30 minutes or refrigerate overnight. Serve at room temperature.

Moroccan Orange and Pomegranate Salad

Makes 6 servings

Blood oranges and pomegranate seeds, along with the freshly ground Moroccan seasonings, make this salad a mysterious adventure.

Tip

Pomegranate seeds are available at Middle Eastern markets and specialty shops.

Variations

Substitute finely chopped red pepper or dried apricots or dried cranberries for the pomegranate seeds.

6	blood oranges, peeled, seeded and thinly sliced	6
1 tbsp	Ras el Hanout (page 50) or store-bought	15 mL
1	small red onion, thinly sliced	1
¼ cup	fresh pomegranate seeds (see Tip, left)	60 mL
3 tbsp	coarsely chopped black olives	45 mL
2 tbsp	chopped fresh mint	30 mL
¼ cup	Lemon Ginger Dressing (see below)	60 mL
¼ cup	Dukkah (page 163) or chopped pistachio nuts, optional	60 mL

1. Line the bottom of a shallow serving dish with orange slices, overlapping if necessary. Sprinkle ras el hanout over top. Separate red onion slices into rings and arrange over orange slices. Distribute pomegranate seeds, olives and mint over orange and onion slices.

2. Drizzle Lemon Ginger Dressing over salad. Cover and let stand at room temperature for 1 to 2 hours. Just before serving, taste and adjust seasoning and garnish with Dukkah, if using.

Lemon Ginger Dressing

Makes ½ cup (125 mL)

Lemon and ginger make a refreshing combination in this dressing. Use it with grilled vegetables and even fruit.

¼ cup	avocado or olive oil	60 mL
3 tbsp	tamari or soy sauce	45 mL
2 tbsp	freshly squeezed lemon juice	30 mL
1 to 2	cloves garlic, minced	1 to 2
1 tbsp	chopped candied ginger	15 mL

1. In a jar with lid or small bowl, combine oil, tamari, lemon juice, garlic and ginger. Shake or whisk to mix well.

Pomegranate and Orange-Glazed Eggplant

Makes 4 to 6 servings

Served warm or at room temperature, this mélange of roasted eggplant and red bell peppers is delicious over a bed of baby spinach or with couscous or rice as a light lunch or side dish.

- Preheat oven to 375°F (190°C)
- 13- by 9-inch (33 by 23 cm) baking pan, lightly oiled

2	eggplants	2
1	red bell pepper, cut into eighths	1
2 tbsp	avocado or olive oil	30 mL
1 cup	finely chopped onions	250 mL
2	cloves garlic, finely chopped	2
1 cup	freshly squeezed orange juice	250 mL
1	piece (1 inch/2.5 cm) candied ginger, finely chopped	1
3 tbsp	soy sauce	45 mL
3 tbsp	Pomegranate Molasses (page 172) or store-bought	45 mL
1 tbsp	rice vinegar	15 mL

1. Remove the blossom end from the eggplants and peel away the skin in strips, leaving some thin strips of skin on each. Cut eggplants in half and each half in 3 wedges. Arrange wedges, skin side down, along with red pepper pieces in a single layer in prepared baking pan. Set aside.

2. Meanwhile, in a saucepan, heat oil over medium heat. Add onions and garlic and cook, stirring occasionally, for 7 minutes or until soft. Add orange juice and bring to a boil, stirring occasionally. Stir in ginger, soy sauce, molasses and rice vinegar and simmer for 1 to 2 minutes.

3. Pour orange glaze over vegetables in the pan. Cover with foil and bake in preheated oven for 40 minutes. Remove foil, turn vegetables over and bake for 15 to 20 minutes or until vegetables are soft and glaze is bubbly.

Roasted Mediterranean Vegetable and Lentil Salad

Makes 4 servings

In summer the grill is easy and fast for cooking vegetables. Use an oiled basket or skewer the veggies whole to grill, then cut into serving-size bites. When roasted, the plums morph into a tart-sweet dressing.

- **Preheat oven to 375°F (190°C)**
- **Rimmed baking sheet, lightly oiled**

2	black plums, cut into eights	2
2	carrots, split lengthwise	2
1	red bell pepper, cut into eighths	1
1	onion, cut into eighths	1
2	cauliflower florets, thinly sliced	2
	Sea salt or freshly ground black pepper	
4 tbsp	avocado or olive oil, divided	60 mL
2 cups	seasonal greens	500 mL
2	medium tomatoes, cut into quarters	2
1	can (14 oz/398 mL) lentils, rinsed and drained	1
2 tbsp	Coriander Pesto (page 41) or Mediterranean Pesto (page 46)	30 mL
2 tbsp	balsamic vinegar	30 mL

1. On prepared baking sheet, combine plums, carrots, bell pepper, onion and cauliflower slices. Season to taste with salt and pepper. Toss with 2 tbsp (30 mL) of the oil. Bake in preheated oven for 40 minutes or until soft and brown on the edges. Let cool slightly.

2. In a salad bowl, combine seasonal greens, tomatoes, lentils and roasted vegetables and pan juices. In a bowl or jar with lid, whisk or shake remaining oil, pesto and vinegar. Drizzle over salad ingredients. Taste and add salt and pepper as required.

Beverages and Sweets

Beverages

Sweets

Apricot Almond Feta Smoothie

Makes 1 to 2 servings

The yogurt and cheese in this drink add protein and calcium.

● **Blender**

½ cup	Almond Milk (page 203) or store-bought	125 mL
¼ cup	plain yogurt	60 mL
4	apricots, halved	4
1	banana, cut into chunks	1
3 tbsp	crumbled feta cheese	45 mL
¼ tsp	Ground Moroccan Spice Blend (page 44)	1 mL

1. In a blender, combine almond milk, yogurt, apricots, banana, cheese and spice blend. Secure lid and blend (from low to high if using a variable speed blender) until smooth.

Almond Date Smoothie

Makes 2 to 3 servings

Almonds and dates are a classic combination for tagines, desserts and drinks.

● **Blender**

¾ cup	Almond Milk (page 203) or store-bought	175 mL
¼ cup	pitted dates	60 mL
2 tbsp	chopped almonds or pecans	30 mL
3 tbsp	cream cheese	45 mL
1	banana, cut into chunks	1
⅛ tsp	ground cinnamon	0.5 mL
Pinch	ground nutmeg	Pinch

1. In a blender, combine almond milk, dates, almonds, cream cheese, banana, cinnamon and nutmeg. Secure lid and blend (from low to high if using a variable speed blender) until smooth.

Almond Milk

Makes 2 cups (500 mL)

Raw, natural almonds give a delicate and sweet almond flavor to the "milk." Use it as a substitute for cow's milk in most recipes.

Tips

Be sure to bring the water to a boil before making the milk. Boiling destroys many water-bound bacteria.

Use a sterilized pint (2 cups/500 mL) jar.

● **Blender or food processor**

1 cup	finely chopped almonds	250 mL
1 tbsp	finely chopped dates	15 mL
1 tbsp	flaxseeds	15 mL
1	piece (1 inch/2.5 cm) vanilla bean	1
2 cups	boiling water	500 mL

1. In a clean jar with a lid, combine almonds, dates, flaxseeds, vanilla bean and water. Shake well and let cool in the jar.

2. In a blender or food processor, process until ingredients are liquefied.

3. Store in a clean jar with a lid in the refrigerator for up to 3 days. Shake well before using.

Fruited Fig Smoothie

Makes 2 servings

Fresh figs make this smoothie a Mediterranean delight but you can omit them when they are not available and use dried instead.

● **Blender**

½ cup	peach or apple juice	125 mL
	Juice of ½ lemon	
2	figs	2
2	apricots, halved	2
1	peach, halved	1
1	plum, halved	1

1. In a blender, combine peach juice, lemon juice, figs, apricots, peach and plum. Secure lid and blend (from low to high if using a variable speed blender) until smooth.

Moroccan Iced Coffee

**Makes
2 servings**

This drink is a great
summer cooler and after
dinner drink. Try it hot
instead of chilled.

2 cups	hot strong brewed coffee	500 mL
1 to
2 tbsp	lightly packed brown sugar	15 to
30 mL
1 tsp	Ground Moroccan Spice Blend
(page 44)	5 mL
¼ cup	plain yogurt	60 mL
3 tbsp	sweetened condensed milk	45 mL
¼ tsp	vanilla extract	1 mL
	Ice cubes	

1. In a glass jug or jar, combine coffee, brown sugar to
   taste and spice blend. Whisk or shake to dissolve the
   sugar and let cool.

2. In a bowl, combine yogurt, sweetened condensed milk
   and vanilla. Add to coffee and whisk or shake. Taste
   and add more spice, brown sugar or condensed milk
   if needed. Chill in the refrigerator for several hours or
   until cold. Whisk or shake and serve over ice.

Moroccan Mint Tea

**Makes
2 to 4 cups
(500 mL to
1 L) tea**

Throughout the Middle
East, pots of invigorating
tea are made with
fresh mint and liberally
sweetened.

Tip

For a true Moroccan-flavored
tea, spearmint is used
but peppermint may be
substituted if the steeping
time is shortened to 3 to
4 minutes.

	Boiling water	
1 heaping
tbsp	dried green tea or 1 green tea bag	15 mL
20	fresh spearmint sprigs (approx.)
(see Tip, left)	20
¼ to
½ cup	granulated sugar	60 to
125 mL

1. Rinse a teapot with boiling water and pour the water
   out. Add green tea and enough spearmint to loosely
   fill the pot about three-quarters full. Add at least
   ¼ cup (60 mL) sugar and fill the pot with boiling
   water.

2. Cover and steep for 5 minutes. Add 2 or 3 mint sprigs
   to each glass and strain tea into the glasses.

Orange Flower Smoothie

Makes 2 servings

Orange flower water is much more delicate in flavor, but if not available, use orange juice.

Tip

See Orange Flower Water Substitute, page 211.

● **Blender**

1 cup	plain yogurt	250 mL
3 tbsp	cold water	45 mL
3 tbsp	orange flower water (see Tip, left)	45 mL
½ cup	fresh or frozen strawberries	125 mL
	Honey or sugar to taste	
2	fresh mint sprigs	2

1. In a blender, combine yogurt, water, orange flower water and strawberries. Secure lid and blend (from low to high if using a variable speed blender) until smooth.

2. Pour into glasses, sweeten to taste and garnish with mint sprigs.

Pomegranate-Orange Smoothie

Makes 2 servings

Street vendors sell pure pomegranate or pomegranate and orange blend juices from their mobile carts and from stalls in the markets. This is a North American smoothie made with traditional fruits of North Africa.

● **Blender**

¾ cup	freshly squeezed orange juice	175 mL
2 tbsp	freshly squeezed lemon juice	30 mL
2	plums, quartered	2
½ cup	pomegranate seeds	125 mL
½ cup	pitted black cherries	125 mL

1. In a blender, combine orange juice, lemon juice, plums, pomegranate seeds and cherries. Secure lid and blend (from low to high if using a variable speed blender) until smooth.

Almond Orange Cake with Apricot Coulis

Makes 1 cake

Desserts in North Africa are not a part of daily meals. Fruit is plentiful and often served plain, stuffed, stewed, or with a light syrup or sauce at the end of a meal. Pastries, ices and cookies or deep-fried delicacies, puddings, jams and preserves are part of the dessert tradition all over the Middle East and take advantage of typical Moroccan ingredients: honey, cinnamon, almonds, orange or rose flower waters, lemons and spice blends. This no-sugar cake is very moist and if undercooked, will be more like a pudding.

- **Preheat oven to 375°F (190°C)**
- **9-inch (23 cm) cake tin, lightly greased**

5	eggs, at room temperature	5
⅔ cup	granulated sugar	150 mL
¾ cup	ground almonds	175 mL
¼ cup	fine bread crumbs	60 mL
1 tbsp	grated orange zest	15 mL
2 tbsp	orange flower water or Orange Flower Water Substitute (page 211)	30 mL
½ tsp	Ground Moroccan Spice Blend (page 44)	2 mL

1. In a large bowl, using electric beater, beat eggs until light and frothy. Gradually beat in sugar.

2. With beaters on low, beat in one at a time and beating well after each addition, almonds, bread crumbs, orange zest, orange flower water and spice blend. Scrape batter into prepared tin. Bake in preheated oven for 45 minutes. Let cool in the tin on a cooling rack. Tip tin upside down over a serving plate to turn out.

Apricot Coulis

Makes 2½ cups (625 mL)

This is always a good sauce to make for finishing off desserts or to use in other recipes as a sweetener.

10	fresh apricots, pitted and cut into quarters	10
3	navel oranges, peeled and chopped	3
1	fresh lemon, peeled and chopped	1
1½ cups	lightly packed brown sugar	375 mL
1	piece (2 inch/5 cm) vanilla bean, split	1
2 tbsp	dried lavender buds, optional	30 mL
½ tsp	ground coriander	2 mL
½ tsp	ground cinnamon	2 mL

1. In a saucepan, combine apricots, oranges, lemon, brown sugar, vanilla bean, lavender, if using, coriander and cinnamon. Bring to a boil over medium-high heat. Reduce heat and simmer, stirring occasionally, for 1½ hours or until thick.

2. Let cool and press through a fine sieve. Use immediately or store in a clean jar with a lid in the refrigerator for up to 1 month.

Apricot Whole-Grain Sesame Bars

Makes about 16 bars

Great to have on hand for snacks and those days when there is no time for breakfast.

- **Preheat oven to 350°F (180°C)**
- **9-inch (23 cm) square baking pan, lightly oiled**

¼ cup	liquid honey	60 mL
⅓ cup	butter	75 mL
1 tsp	grated orange zest	5 mL
2 tbsp	freshly squeezed orange juice	30 mL
1 cup	whole wheat flour	250 mL
½ cup	wheat bran or buckwheat flour	125 mL
1 cup	large-flake rolled oats	250 mL
1	apple, grated	1
½ cup	chopped dried apricots	125 mL
½ cup	slivered almonds	125 mL
¼ cup	sesame seeds	60 mL

1. In a small saucepan, combine honey, butter, and orange zest and juice. Heat over medium-low heat until butter is melted. Set aside.

2. In a large bowl, whisk together whole wheat flour, bran and rolled oats. Stir in apple, apricots, almonds and sesame seeds. Pour honey mixture into dry ingredients and stir until well blended.

3. Scrape into prepared pan. Bake in preheated oven for 35 minutes or until golden brown. Let cool completely in pan on a rack. Cut into squares. Store bars in an airtight container at room temperature for up to 3 days.

Date and Nut Bars

Makes about 16 bars

The sweetness of the dates means very little extra sugar is needed in this healthy bar recipe.

Variation

Use 1 cup (250 mL) chopped dates and 1 cup (250 mL) chopped figs instead of dates only.

- **Preheat oven to 350°F (180°C)**
- **9-inch (23 cm) square baking pan, lightly oiled**

2 cups	chopped fresh or dried dates	500 mL
½ cup	apple juice	125 mL
¾ cup	whole wheat flour	175 mL
¼ cup	buckwheat flour	60 mL
1 cup	large-flake rolled oats	250 mL
2 tbsp	unsweetened cocoa powder	30 mL
½ tsp	salt	2 mL
¼ cup	chopped walnuts or pecans	60 mL
6 tbsp	butter, at room temperature	90 mL
1 tbsp	lightly packed brown sugar	15 mL
¼ cup	confectioner's (icing) sugar, optional	60 mL

1. In a saucepan, combine dates and apple juice. Bring to a boil over high heat. Cover, reduce heat and simmer for 5 minutes or until dates are soft. Let cool slightly.

2. Meanwhile, in a bowl, whisk together whole wheat flour, buckwheat flour, rolled oats, cocoa and salt. Stir in walnuts.

3. Using a wooden spoon, beat butter and brown sugar into dates. Scrape date mixture into flour mixture and beat well.

4. Press into prepared pan. Bake in preheated oven for 20 minutes for a moist chewy bar. Bake longer (about 25 minutes) for a drier, cake-like bar. Let cool completely in pan on a rack. Dust with confectioner's sugar, if using. Cut into squares. Store bars in an airtight container at room temperature for up to 3 days.

Gingered Fruit Tagine

Makes 3 cups (750 mL)

Make this easy compote when fresh fruit is plentiful and serve with yogurt or toss with cooked rice for a healthy rice pudding.

Tips

Use a combination of fresh apricots, nectarines, peaches, plums, cherries, blueberries and other fresh berries.

Store, tightly covered, in the refrigerator for up to 5 days.

● **Small tagine**

1 lb	fresh fruit, peeled and pitted (see Tips, left)	500 g
¼ cup	sliced dried apricots	60 mL
¼ cup	chopped fresh or dried dates	60 mL
¼ cup	Pomegranate Molasses (page 172) or brown rice syrup	60 mL
2 tsp	minced fresh gingerroot	10 mL
2 tbsp	freshly squeezed lemon juice	30 mL

1. Cut larger fruit into quarters and smaller fruit into halves. In the bottom of a flameproof tagine, combine fresh fruit, apricots, dates, molasses and ginger. Cover and cook over medium-low heat for 10 minutes or until juices release and fruit is slightly tender.

2. Stir in lemon juice and cook, stirring constantly, for 2 minutes or until fruit is soft. Serve warm or chilled (the mixture will thicken when cooled).

Minted Watermelon in Orange Flower Water

**Makes
4 servings**

Orange flower water is
available online or at
Middle Eastern stores,
and it is best for these
recipes. Use the recipe
below as a substitute
if necessary.

Tip

Moroccans use spearmint to
flavor many dishes. I actually
prefer peppermint, but here it
overpowers the delicate taste
of watermelon and orange
flower water.

2½ cups	1-inch (2.5 cm) cubes or balls seeded watermelon	625 mL
½ cup	orange flower water or substitute (see below)	125 mL
3 tbsp	chopped fresh spearmint (see Tip, left)	45 mL

1. In a bowl, combine watermelon, orange flower water and peppermint. Serve immediately.

Orange Flower Water Substitute

**Makes ½ cup
(125 mL)**

Both rosewater and
orange flower water are
available at Moroccan or
Middle Eastern food stores,
but I think that this easy
and flavorful alternative is
a versatile substitution. It is
not as delicate as the true
water made from orange
flowers, but it works
in baked goods and in
the Minted Watermelon
recipe above.

¼ cup	water	60 mL
1 tsp	orange zest	5 mL
¼ cup	freshly squeezed orange juice	60 mL
1 tbsp	orange liqueur	15 mL

1. In a bowl, combine water, orange zest, orange juice and orange liqueur. Use immediately or store in a jar with a tight-fitting lid for up to 3 days in the refrigerator.

Sources

Bibliography

Basac, Ghillie. *Tagines and Couscous*. New York: Ryland, Peters & Small, 2010.

Benghiat, Suzy. *Middle Eastern Cooking*. USA: Harmony Books, 1984.

Crocker, Pat. *The Vegetarian Cook's Bible*. Toronto: Robert Rose Inc., 2007.

Henry, Diana. *Crazy Water Pickled Lemons*. London: Mitchell Beazley, 2002.

Morse, Kitty. *North Africa: The Vegetarian Table*. San Francisco: Chronicle Books, 1996.

Roden, Claudia. *A Book of Middle Eastern Food*. London: Thomas Nelson & Sons, 1968.

Woodward, Sarah. *Tastes of North Africa*. New York: Hippocrene Books Inc., 1999.

—. *The Food of Morocco*. Vancouver: Whitecap Books, 2008.

Equipment and Ingredients

Tagine Equipment

There are several tagines available online and at kitchen or department stores. The following is a list of equipment that is available in either Canada or the United States, or both countries.

Emile Henry (formerly Emile Henri)
Tagines and mortar and pestles
(in various colors).
www.emilehenry.com/emile-henry

Fantes Kitchen Wares Shop
Handmade, traditional terra cotta tagines.
www.fantes.com

Le Creuset
www.lecreuset.com

Maxwell & Williams
Tagines and mortar and pestles.
www.maxwellandwilliams.com

Staub
www.staubusa.com

Couscoussière Pots

Cuisinox, 3 piece, stainless steel
www.cuisinox.com

Fantes Kitchen Wares Shop
3-piece, hand-hammered copper and stainless steel
www.fantes.com

Williams-Sonoma
3 piece, hand-hammered copper
www.williams-sonoma.com

Spices and Oil

There is a wide array of whole and blended spices available at bulk, health and specialty food stores as well as online. Get to know ethnic food retail outlets in your community, where you can purchase whole fresh spices for the spice blend recipes in this book. Here is a short list of online resources:

Arvinda's Indian Spice Blends
Indian spice blends from family recipes, freshly ground and blended; no oils, additives, preservatives or fillers; several masala blends including Garam and Tikka; available in Canada and U.S.A.
www.arvindas.com

Frontier Herbs and Spices
Organic, non-irradiated herbs and whole spices and Garam Masala spice blend, mortar and pestles.
www.frontiercoop.com

Silk Road Spices
Whole spices and spice blends, no fillers, artificial colors or preservatives; a wide variety of blends including Turkish Bahrat, Ethiopian Berbere, Garam Masala, Ras el Hanout and Za'atar.
www.silkroadspices.ca

Smoke Fine Foods
Smoked spices including Grilling Spices, Roasted Garlic, Paprika and smoked couscous and rice.
www.smokefinefoods.com

Zamouri Spices
Spice blends including Baharat-Arabian Style, Berbere-Ethiopian, Charmoula, Harissa and others.
www.zamourispices.com

Olivado
Pioneered the process of extracting the oil from avocado fruits. Their Avocado Zest® is a cold pressed avocado oil and lemons, which is perfect for tagine cooking.
www.olivado.com

Index

Library and Archives Canada Cataloguing in Publication

Crocker, Pat
150 best tagine recipes : including tantalizing recipes for spice blends and accompaniments / Pat Crocker.

Includes index.
ISBN 978-0-7788-0279-2

1. Cooking, Moroccan. 2. Cooking, North African. 3. Cookbooks.
I. Title. II. Title: One hundred fifty best tagine recipes.

TX725.M67C76 2011   641.5964   C2011-903183-3